DUET

Poems & Photographs

Poetry by

ELIZABETH BURK

Photographs by

LEO TOUCHET

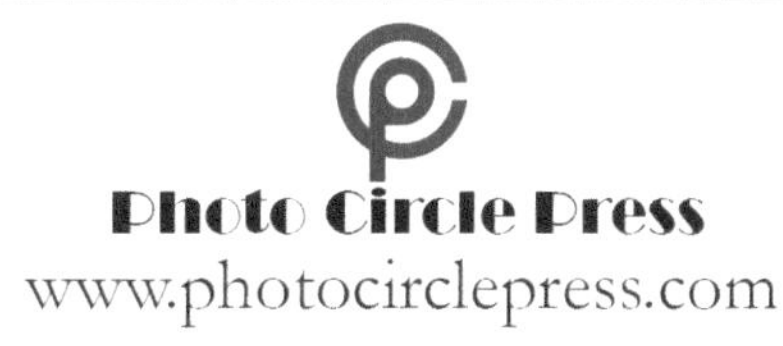

DUET

Poems & Photographs

Elizabeth Burk and Leo Touchet

Design - Leo Touchet

ISBN 979-8-9918323-4-2

Second Edition
July 2025

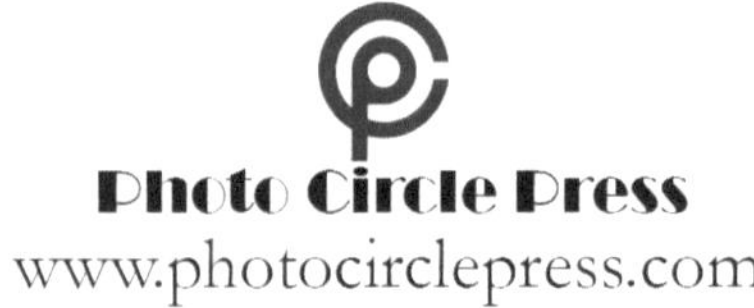

www.photocirclepress.com

For our children:
Carolyn Touchet
Patrick Moner
Justin Burk
Our grandchildren:
Lucy Burk
*Jennifer Goas
Jacqueline Goas
Alec Jacober
Bridgette Jacober
Jared Moner
Isabella Merced
Gyovanni Moner
Our great-grandchildren:
Elle Laffey
Willow Laffey
Joey Laffey

* *Deceased*

CONTENTS

PREFACE / 8 - 9

POEMS / 11 - 55

ACKNOWLEDGEMENTS / 56

PHOTOGRAPH NOTES / 57

ABOUT THE AUTHORS / 58 - 59

POEMS

GOD VISITS LOUISIANA / 11
HUSH OVER ATCHAFALAYA / 13
THE ROAD WIDOW / 15
THREE NUNS / 17
CATECHISM / 19
CATALONIA, 1973 / 21
SOUR TASTE OF PINEAPPLES / 23
PIGEON / 25
AUTUMN IN PARIS / 27
MADAME BELLEFLEUR / 29
RASPUTIN'S PENIS / 31
APRODITE'S HEADACHE / 33
INTOXICATION / 35
READY / 37
MATAMOROS / 39
DESIRE / 41
LINE DANCE / 43
GHOST OF MY FUTURE SELF / 45
ROCKEFELLER CENTER / 47
SILK PAISLEY AND PEARLS / 49*
THE AGING PLAYER / 51
POLAR BEARS IN EXILE / 53
HORIZON / 55

ELIZABETH BURK

Several years ago I began to write poems inspired by my husband Leo's dune photographs. I found it quite a challenge because of their ambiguous, abstract nature. My poems are usually narrative, taken from life experiences, mine or others'–I'm basically a story-teller. But the dunes invited a more reflective, associative, dream-like process. I hid these poems away in a folder.

When Leo suggested the idea of creating a book together—his photos and my poems—I retrieved the poems inspired by his dune photos, and also started writing poems based on images of the people and places he photographed, in most instances reverting back to story-teller mode.

I often share with Leo poems I've written. As our project progressed, he began to comment, "I have just the photograph to go with that poem." Ekphrasis in reverse? Sometimes we argued as to the best photograph for a particular poem. For him, a visual person, the criteria was always the quality of the image; for me, a word person, it was which photograph best expressed the essence of the poem. When I asked him why his favorite photograph was the old man sitting in a chair in Catalonia, Spain, I expected to hear a story about the content of the photo. Instead he answered "because it has black, white and every shade of gray." This answer surprised me, but in turn informed a revision of the poem. In these ways the project became truly interactive and collaborative.

In the process of selecting photographs, I found myself gravitating towards images of older people, reflecting my preoccupation with the process of aging—how aging shapes desire and passion, how it impacts our changing view of ourselves, our involvement with the world. My interest in current socio-cultural issues has also been projected onto some of these images and inspired several of these poems—feminism seeps in, as does religion and politics. Finally, this project represents, for us, art in conversation—we are not only collaborators in life and marriage, we are also now collaborators in co-creating an art form. Hopefully our individual work builds in meaning when placed side by side, his images and my poems conversing with one another.

LEO TOUCHET

My photography career began in 1965 by studying photographs of great photographers like Henri Cartier-Bresson, Eugene Smith, David Seymour and others in the archives of the Museum of Modern Art in New York City. Since then, as a photojournalist, I've worked with writers for numerous publications around the world producing photographs to accompany articles for publication. Some of the journalists complained thst my photographs were taking too much space in the articles, while I always fell back on the old saying that a photograph was worth a thousand words.

A couple of years back, Liz asked me to accompany her to a poetry reading where she and several other poets were planning to read ekphrastic poems. The word sounded more like a rare tropical disease rather than a type of poem, but I was impressed with how the poets were able to write poems inspired by other visual art forms. The poets read poems which were inspired by paintings, and paintings inspired by poems.

In 2017, Liz conceived the idea of having six poets write poems inspired by photographs from my exhibition, *PEOPLE AMONG US*, at the Acadiana Center for the Arts in Lafayette, Louisiana. Each poet selected two photographs from the exhibit and wrote poems inspired by the photographs. The event, *IMAGE TO WORD*, was a poetry reading which took place in the exhibition gallery. It attracted over three hundred people, overflowing the gallery and out into the hallways. This event sparked the idea to do a book together. Having worked for years with journalists, collaborating with a poet on a book was something entirely new to me.

The process of sequencing the book produced some interesting encounters. I'm a visual person, Liz is a word person and we are married. After consulting with friends (referees), we ended with two different versions for the book. My version was sequenced with the photographs and her version was sequenced with the poems. We shipped the two versions to the publisher, who then selected Liz's version for this book. Unlike in journalism, the photographs and poems in this book have equal value.

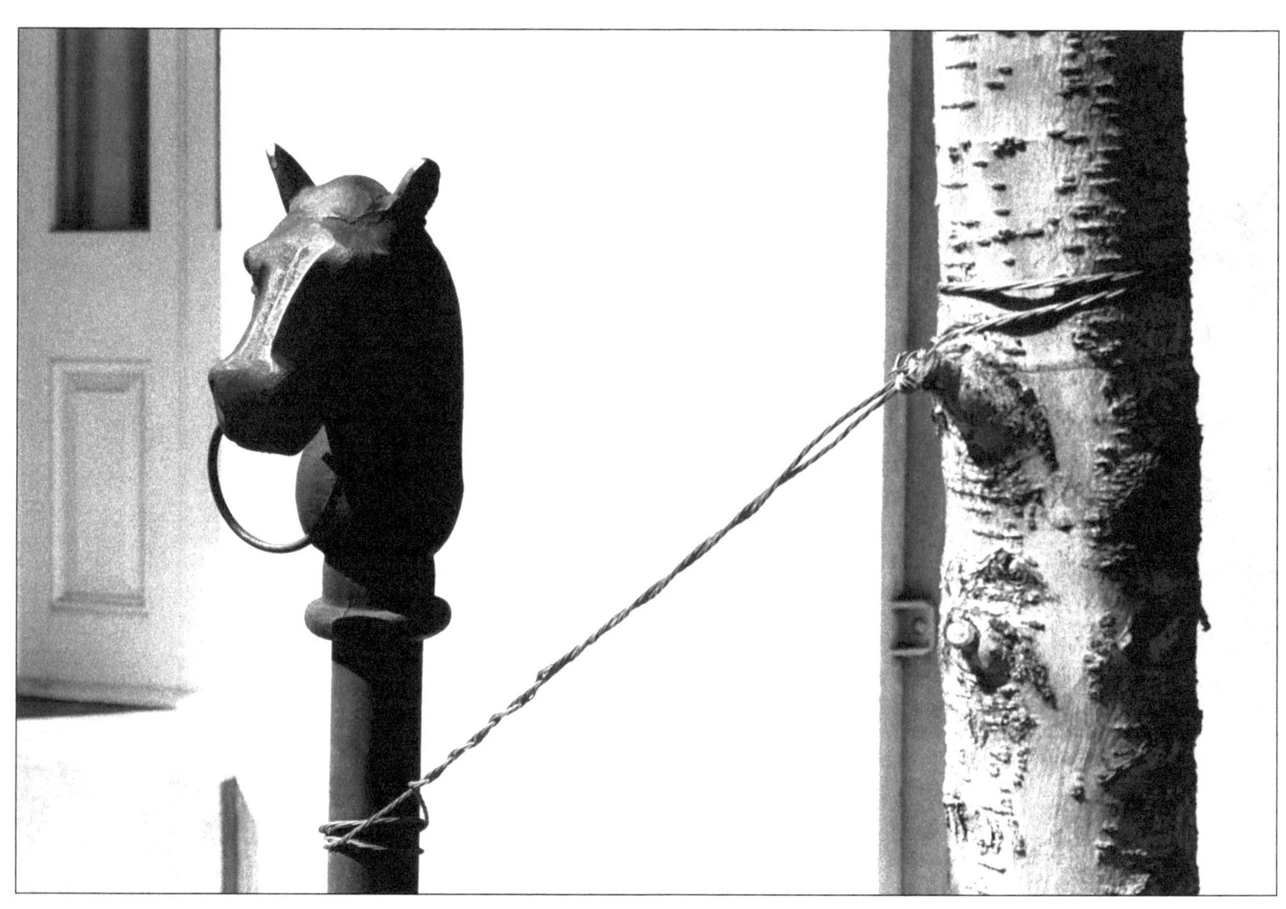

New Orleans, Louisiana 1969

GOD VISITS LOUISIANA, 1860

He rode into town
on a proud prancing
palomino. God held
the reins tight, dismounted,
tied his horse to a post,
went into the nearest saloon,
ordered a few beers

and began bragging
about earlier exploits—
mountains, dinosaurs, men—
then he moved on
to later creations—cotton gin,
steam engine, sewing machine.

Some of the regulars
did not take kindly
to this stranger in their midst
claiming he was God.
They challenged him
to a duel. God was cocky.
I created you, he shouted.

But God had little practice
with the pistol, invented
since he was last challenged.
He called on John, a fast draw,
and said, *Fight my battles, please,*
I'm going back into the saloon.

God was last seen leading
a horse out of town—
a mangy pinto, not
the one he rode in on.

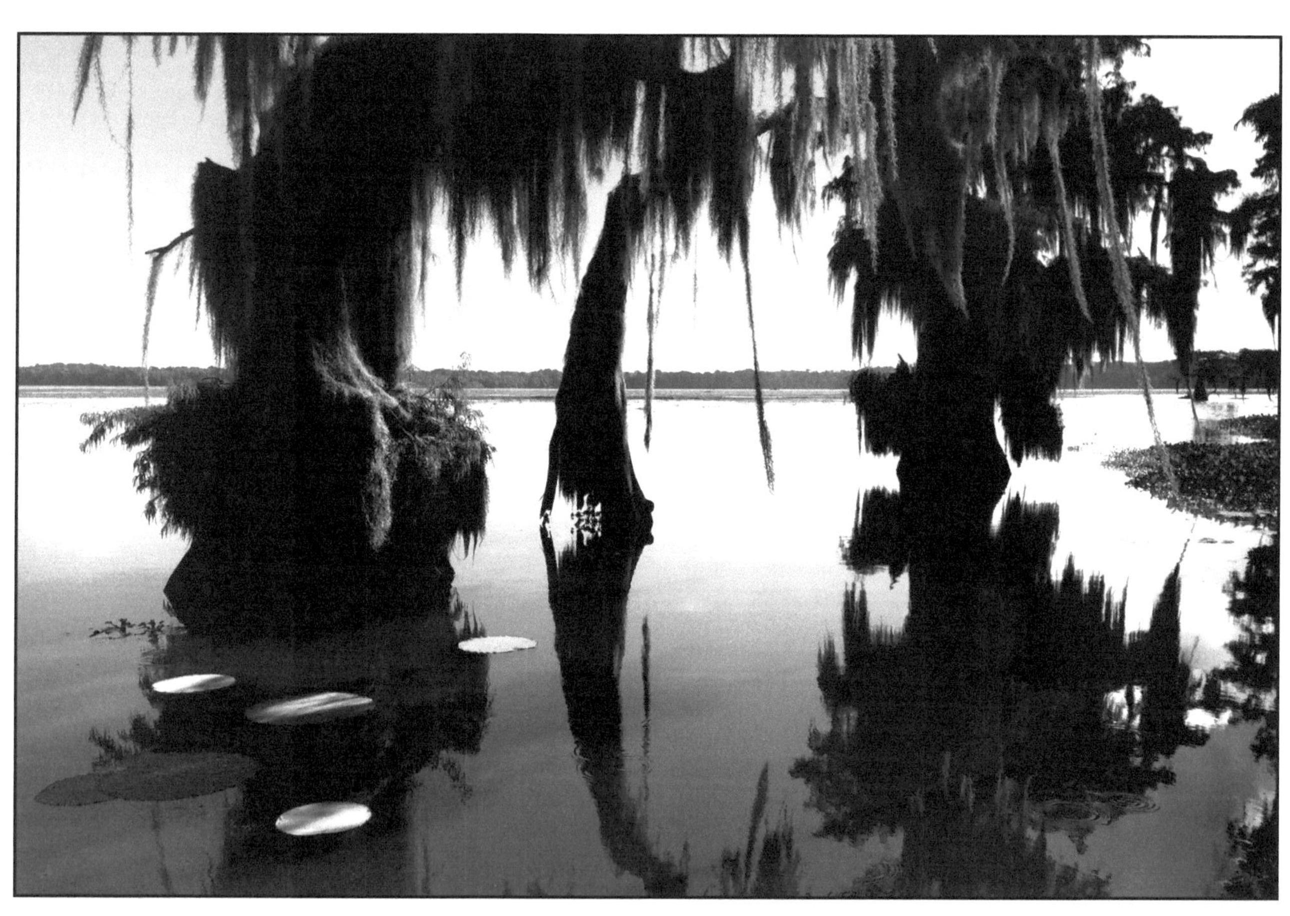

Atchafalaya Basin Swamp, Louisiana 2014

HUSH OVER ATCHAFALAYA

Beyond the ragged camp
a sagging wooden plank stretches back
into the swamp. It is barely dusk, heat melts from
the day, the moisture clings. A weathered outboard

motor murmurs its way through the murky waters
of the bayou. A white heron on the shore watches,
still as dawn; dragonflies hover above. Two baby beavers
peer from their hiding place inside a hollow log.

Around a bend, the river widens,
massive tree trunks rise from the water, ancient limbs
hang heavy with moss. Alligators glide by, grinning
jaws skim the water's surface, their scaly bodies submerged.

Silvery cypress stumps poke through stagnant waters
like fixed bayonets, ghosts of a forgotten war.
In the river's reflections, a hidden universe beckons
as the boat slips through the channel leaving no trace.

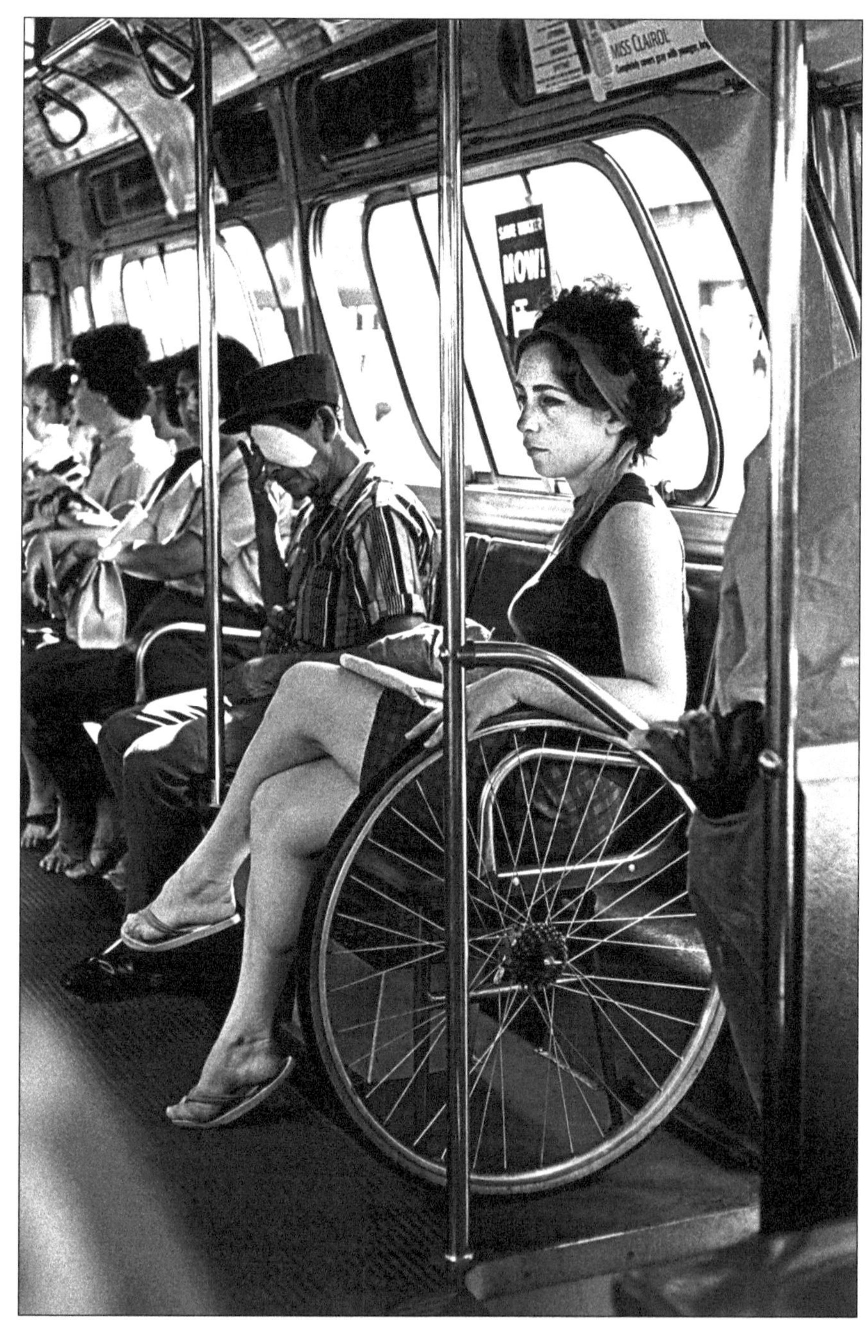

New York, New York 1965

THE ROAD WIDOW

When you are gone
each city you are in
lights up like a neon sign,
beckons like Broadway
dancers and go-go girls.
I see bars, strangers, ex-wives,
imagined worlds
where you loved others
and left, or were left behind.

My body tilts south
where you have gone.
I taste cane sugar,
feel the wilting heat.
I am surrounded
by weepy trees,
gnarled arms reaching out
over sultry swamps
where the murky deep rises
to meet the sky.

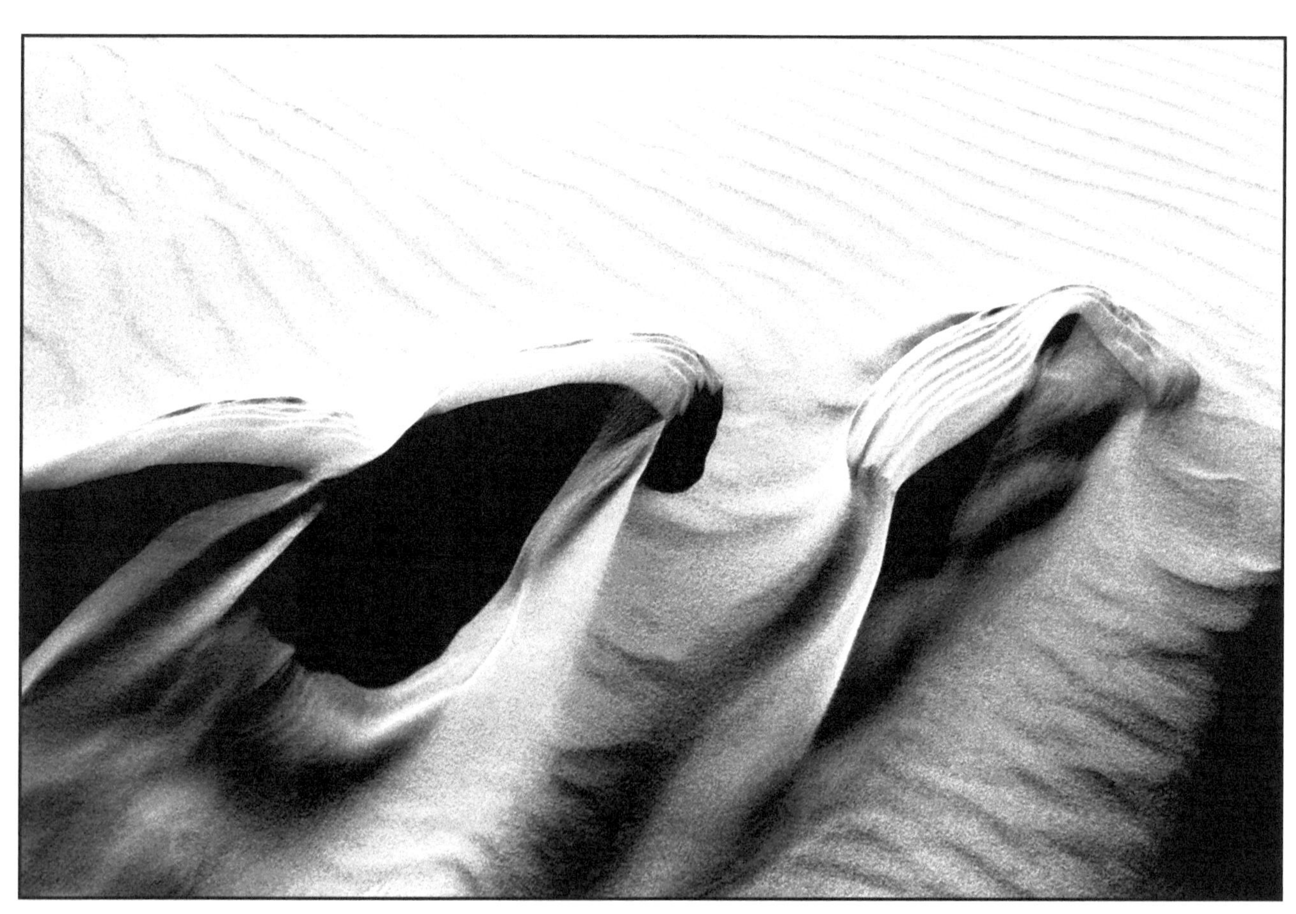

Monahan's Sand Hills State Park, Texas 1994

THREE NUNS

tilted, dizzy from a long
dry day in the desert, lie down
to rest a bit before making their way

home to the monastery tent.
To lighten their burden, they empty
their habits, their hood—long ago

they bleached their egos
in service to suffering.
They lean, exhausted, against

one another, drained from feeding
starving children, comforting
the grieving, tending torn bodies,

their own parched bodies turned
to dust. Only the robes remain,
habits to which they must return.

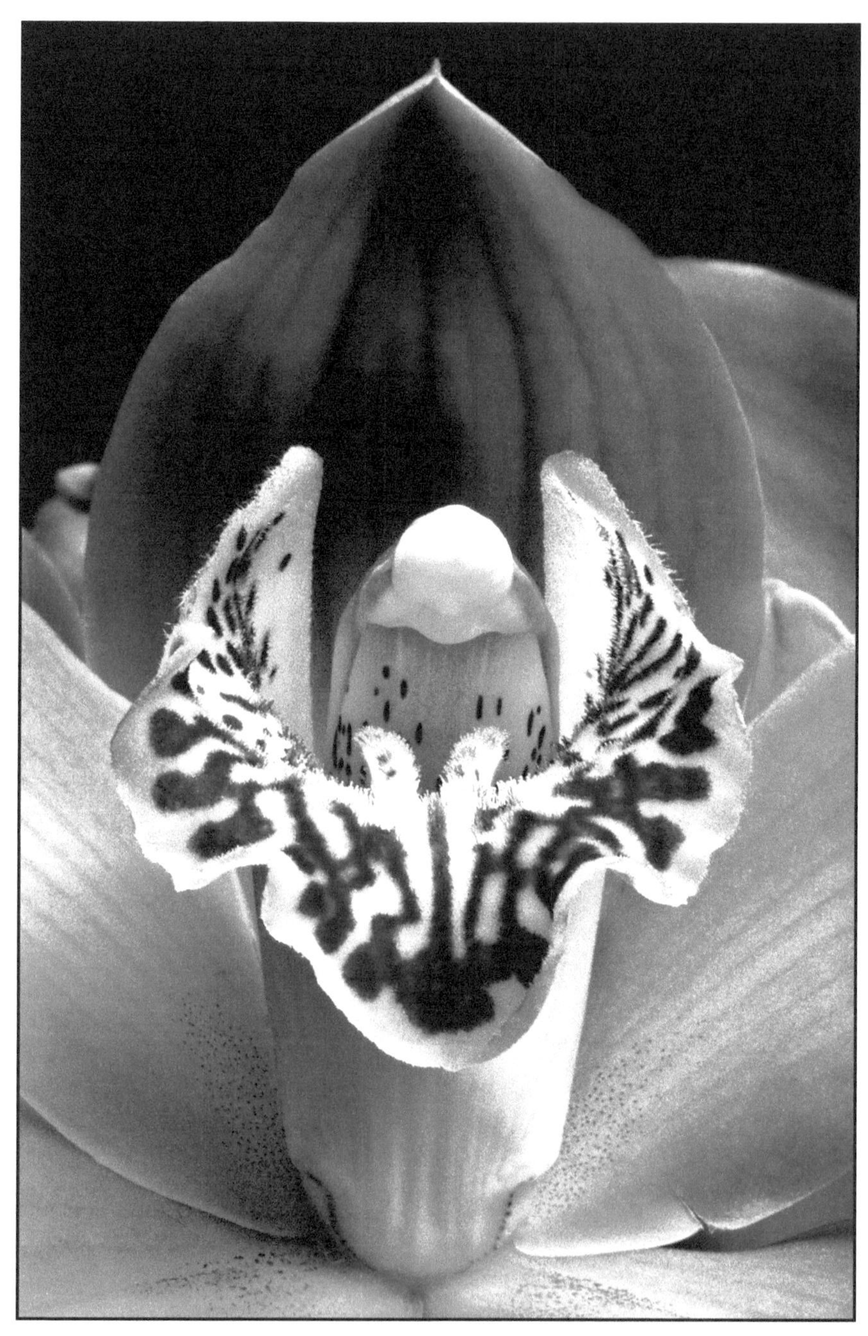

Armonk, New York 2005

CATECHISM

In the schoolyard six stories below our apartment,
nuns with lips straight as rulers, pale eyes glinting
behind steel rims, watched the children at recess.

Priests were equally ominous. Crosses dangled
over large guts, pointing to the place where penises
might be. When the bell rang an eerie silence ensued.

In the streets, the Catholic kids bullied me, told me
I killed Jesus, threatened limbo or even worse,
purgatory. My mother called it nonsense.

I was not reassured. Sunday mornings I envied Catholic girls
in their shiny white dresses, ring of flowers in their hair,
young brides, smug in the knowledge they were forgiven

all sins. I, too, wanted to confess. A playmate led me
on a furtive excursion through massive wooden doors—
inside, echo of bells and organs, solemn swish of black robes,

heads bowed in prayer. A chorus of celestial voices
swelling in unison filled a hollow in my chest—
structure steeped in ritual—compelling, seductive, it beckoned.

Holy, holy, holy. I borrowed rosary beads, learned to chant.
What the hell is this? my father barked when he found them
on the bathroom sink tangled up in his razor and shaving cream.

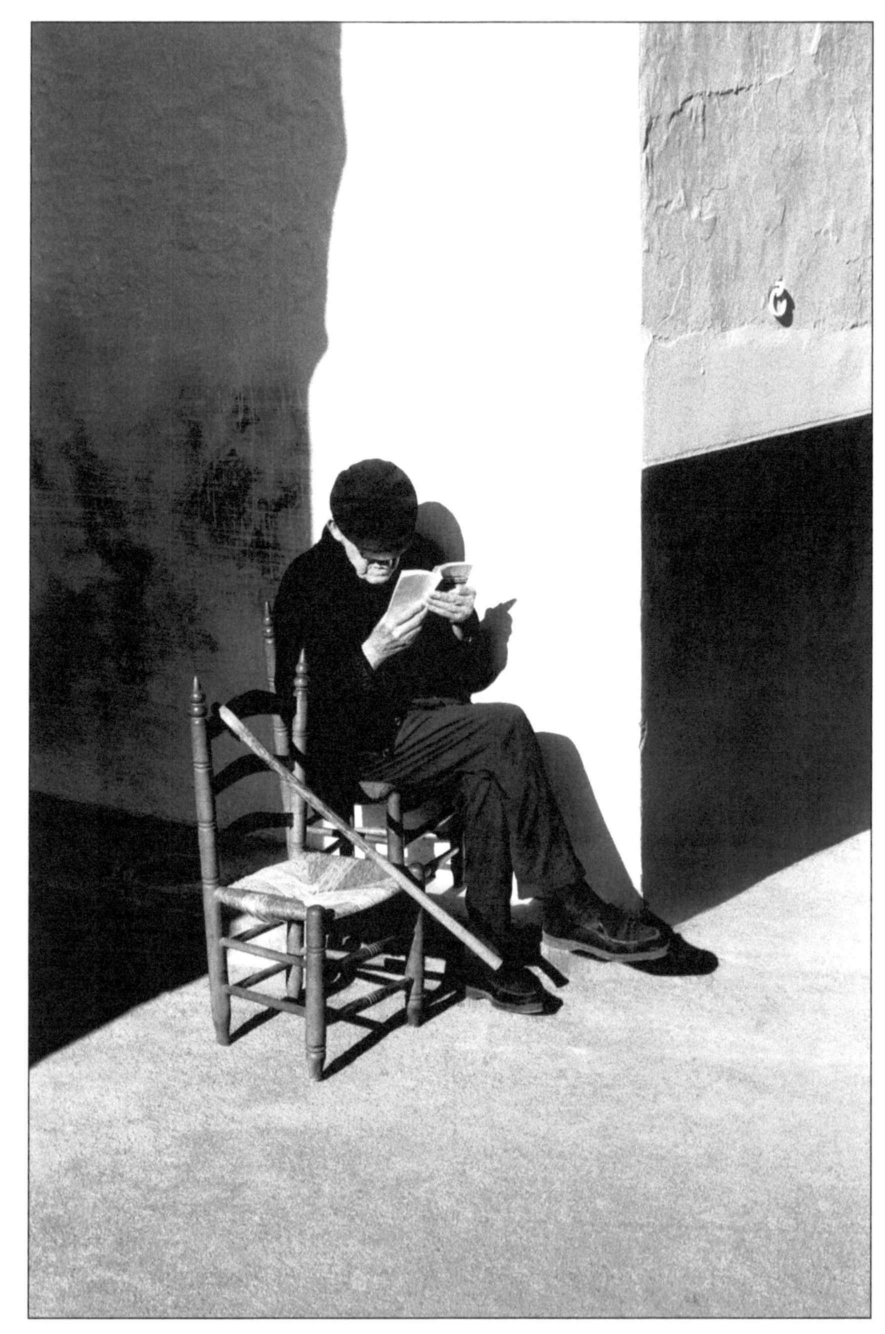

Catalonia, Spain 1973

CATALONIA, 1973

The old man is reading but his shadow hand holds a gun,
his cane propped against a companion chair he saves for his wife
who was killed 40 years ago during the Spanish Civil War.

His long fingers obscure the title – impossible to tell
if he's holding a pamphlet of pro-Franco propaganda,
Illustrated erotica, or a manifesto on Catalan independence.

He reminds me of my father, an armchair activist
who sat nightly under a map of the Soviet Union
he had taped to our cracked, peeling walls, dozing

over Marxist tomes, copies of The Daily Worker
urging workers of the world to unite—waking to extol
Stalin's massacres for the sake of the cause.

Always the cause. The old man too dozes, his dreams
mingle with memories—the red dress his wife wore
to rallies, their fevered talks into the night ending

in passionate embraces, the speeches, screaming crowds,
the blood-stained streets, the in-fighting between factions—
on the same side—so violent that the fight for freedom

against fascism collapsed under the weight of its own
divided dogmas. Sometimes the old man wonders
if it matters what side they were fighting for. Time

is the enemy now. He still misses his wife
and his son, now Franco's political prisoner
in the building where he keeps a lonely vigil.

But the old man, too, is a prisoner of his own shadows, only
his books, his memories to shield him from seeing the pillars
of divided light rising behind his back –one white wall,

one black—while outside the picture frame his dog lies
on the gray concrete beneath them both
each waiting for the other to lead the way home.

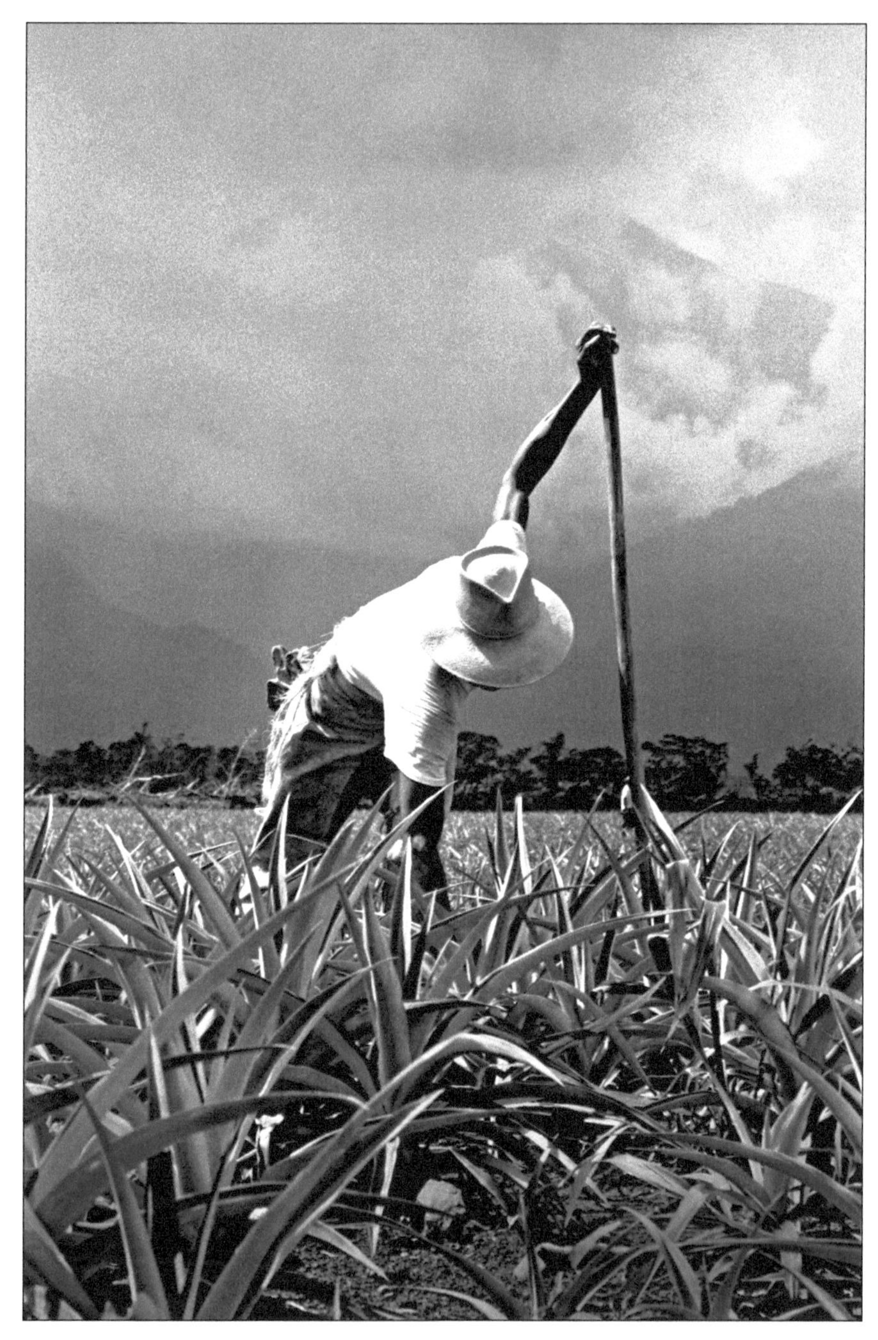

La Ceiba, Honduras 1968

SOUR TASTE OF PINEAPPLES

One arm reaches down
to tug weeds from the earth,
the other raised to roiling sky
hangs on a wooden hoe for balance—
humble trinity, holy triangle—
his aching body, mind, spirit
stark against muted mountains,
eighteen hours hostage to heat,
bones aging fast and brittle,
serving a fruit no longer sweet.
Sweat dries to salt on his lips.

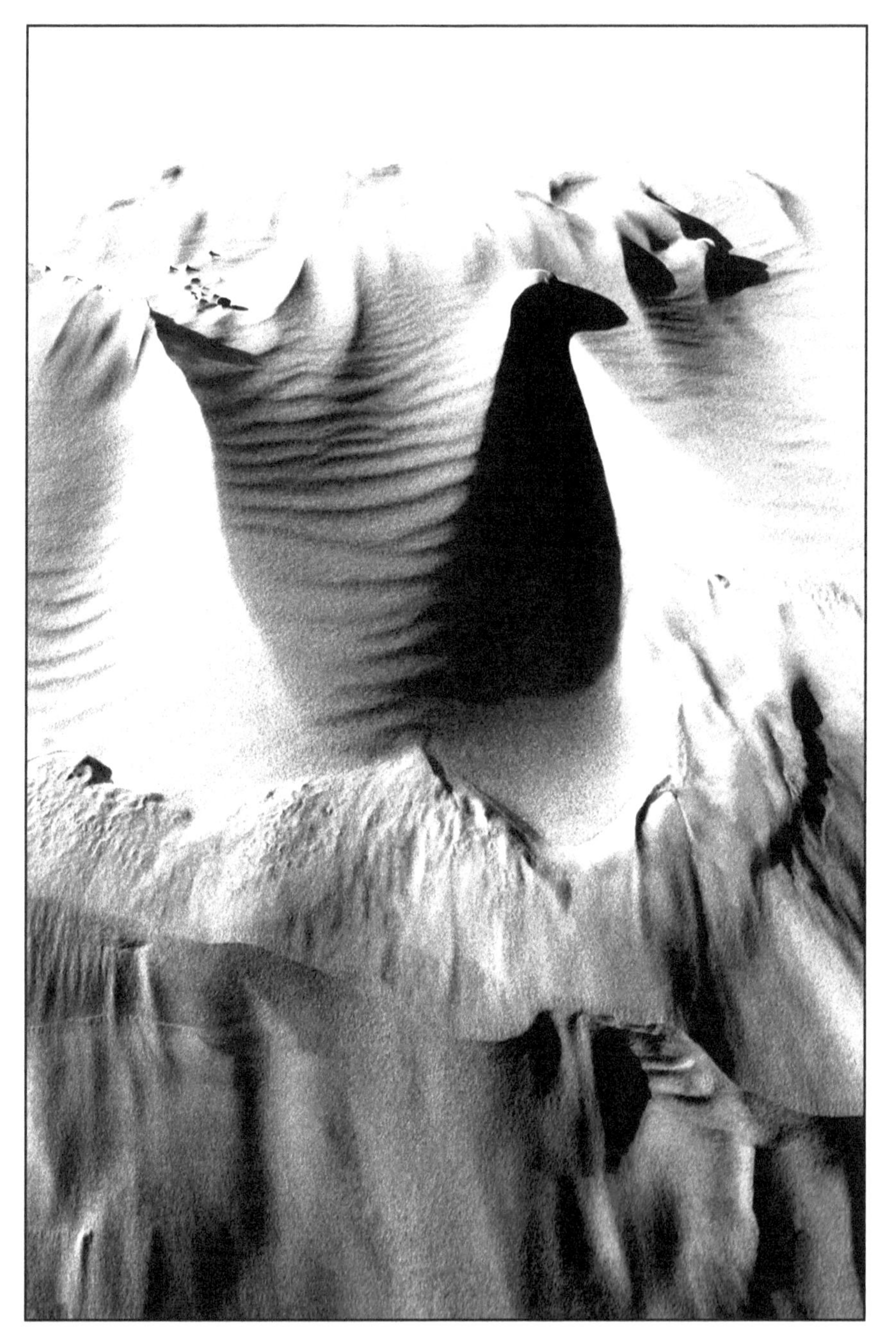

Monahan's Sand Hills State Park, Texas 1994

PIGEON

Headed downtown for a wedding reception,
we see a dead pigeon on the subway platform.
No blood, no visible means of death.

A toddler strapped in stroller points to the pigeon,
asks momma why is it sleeping here? Momma
silently wheels the child away.

Year ago, on a crowded Egyptian beach, four men weave
through the throngs, each carrying a limb of a man
face down. Families gathered continue to play cards,

picnic lunches spread across wooden tables—no one
glances up or makes way. My husband offers medical
assistance but is unable to resuscitate the dead man—we leave

before police arrive. I question our native guide.
In shah-allah, he answers. *That's how we think
of life and death—it's god's will, what will be will be.*

The wedding reception boasts buffet tables—lobster, shrimp,
wine, whiskey, filet mignon, chocolate meringues. The bride
wears white silk, the groom a pigeon-gray suit, white ruffled shirt.

Headed back home, the uptown train station is littered
with wrappers, empty bottles, puddle of vomit, teens
in dreds, old men slumped on benches in disheveled stupors.

Another lone pigeon struts the platform pecking at garbage.
The train arrives, we push our way into a crowded car. The pigeon
hops from foot to foot like a child wanting to board. How long
will it survive in this toxic corridor, I wonder. In shah-allah.

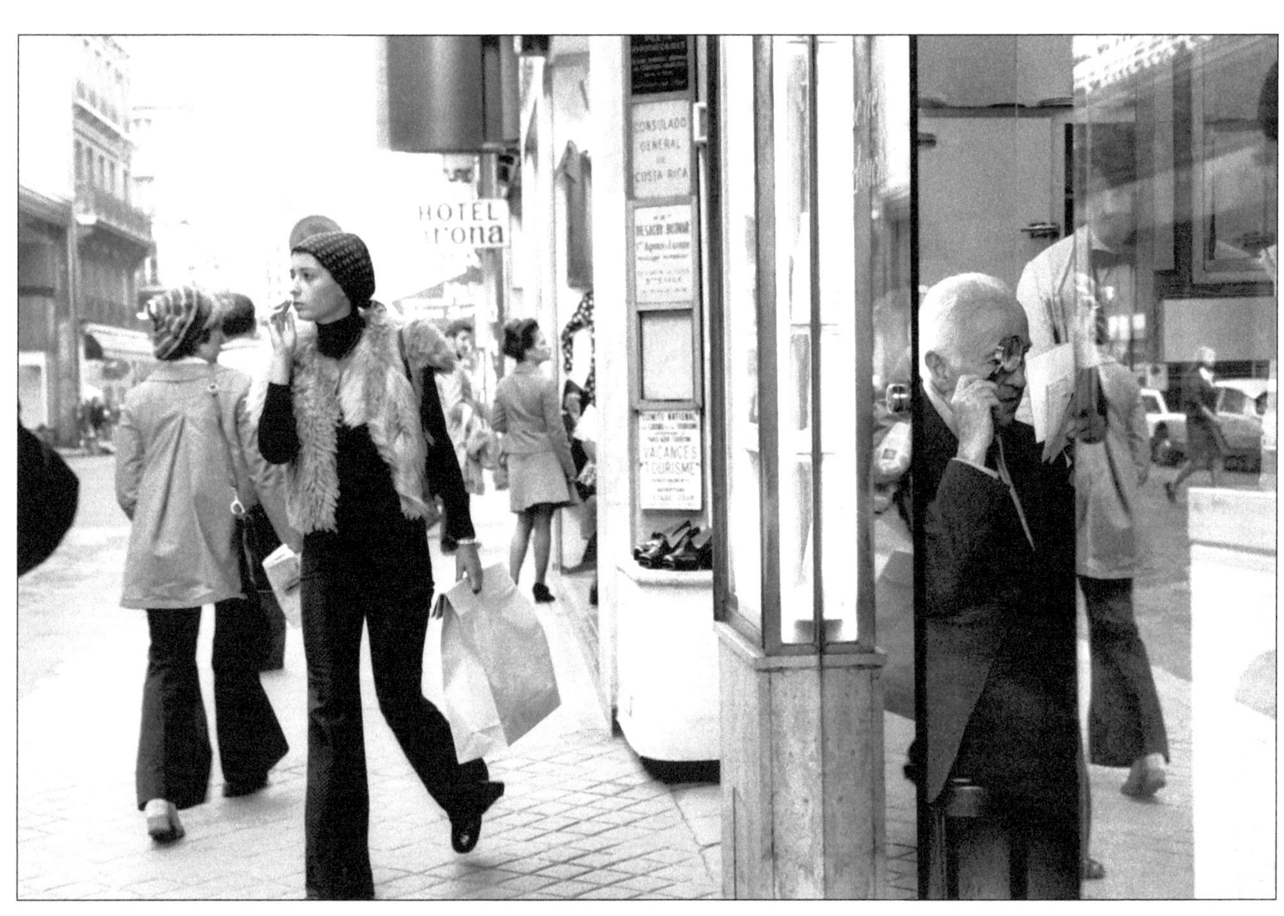

Paris, France 1972

AUTUMN IN PARIS

The gendarme stops us halfway down
the crowded Boulevard St. Germaine.
Mesdemoiselles, he says, motioning
with his stick toward the black briefcase
Lisa carries in her hand. *Arretez,*
s'il vous plaît—Ouvrez!

Stunned, we obey the French police
with lead-lined cape, scowling face.
I think he's asking us to open it,
I say to Lisa whose long blond bangs
hang over her eyes, blue and brimming
with frightened tears.

She bends and opens the ominous case,
displaying a clatter of pipes, brass rings,
the makings of a *plastique*, perhaps?
The gendarme is alarmed, as Lisa waves
her arms, her classroom French dissolving.

There on the boulevard we assemble
the offending instrument of terror—
a bassoon. Lisa rallies, plays a tune
as if to say, there is nothing to fear.

Foreign students stop to stare,
immaculately coiffed Parisiennes
glare, on bridges and boulevards
bombs explode, students riot, war
is in the air, while we American girls
play Vivaldi in the street.

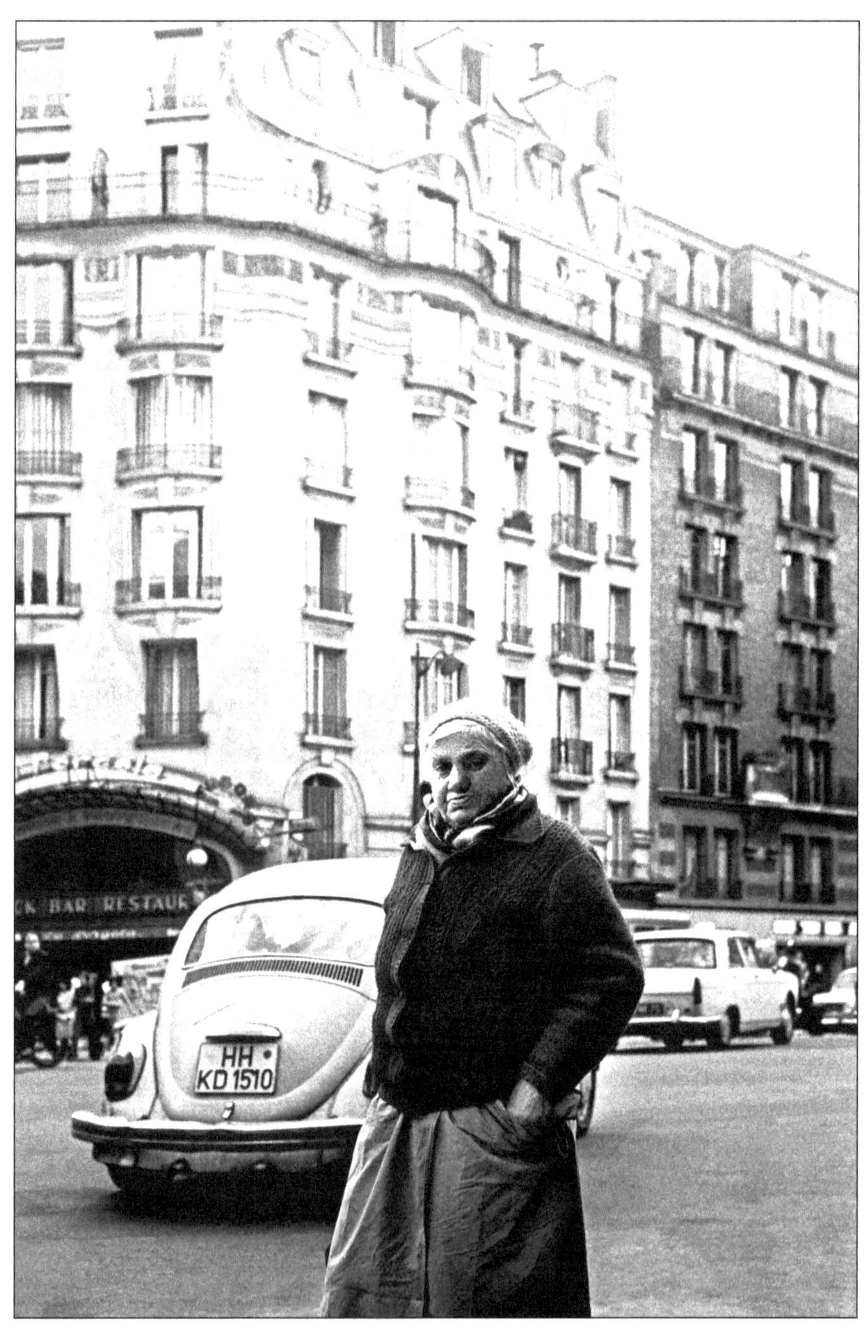

Paris, France 1972

MADAME BELLEFLEUR

Our concierge was constant witness to the chaotic rotation
of roommates, friends, lovers who lived with us in the huge,
elegantly shabby apartment we'd rented on Avenue Montaigne.

On the other side of town, in the Latin Quarter jazz caves
Jessica picked up men, brought them back home. A trail
of clothes—coat, scarf, skirt, sweater, boots, black tights—
led from front door to her bedroom. By morning,

the couple emerged—bleary, hung over, stumbling towards
the coffee pot in the kitchen where we sat smirking, the guy eager
to retreat after a quick cup of instant while Jessica lit a cigarette
and sulked. *Chicas Americanas*, said my Spanish lover, who lived

in my room at the end of the corridor, scandalized by our wanton ways.
Pendeja, he called her, Spanish for pubic hair. Secretly, we called her
clitorissima. Evenings, Jessica hunkered silently in our living room
reading Newsweek, drinking scotch, electric heater tucked between

her legs. When MaryAnn got pregnant, Jessica suggested a plane trip
to Morocco, a taxi to the nearest clinic. Instead, MaryAnn's lover
found a local doc who inserted sharp objects inside her, sent her home
to call him when she bled. But her cervix closed up like a virgin's.

A week later, all-knowing Mme Bellefleur handed her a note
with a doctor's name, an address in Rome. Go, she said, *before*
it's too late. When MaryAnn returned to Paris, Mme Bellefleur
asked if her Roman holiday went well. *Oui, Madame*, MaryAnn replied,

although I missed seeing the Pope—maybe next time.
Mme Bellefleur frowned, replied, *Mais non, mademoiselle,*
we must hope there is not a next time.

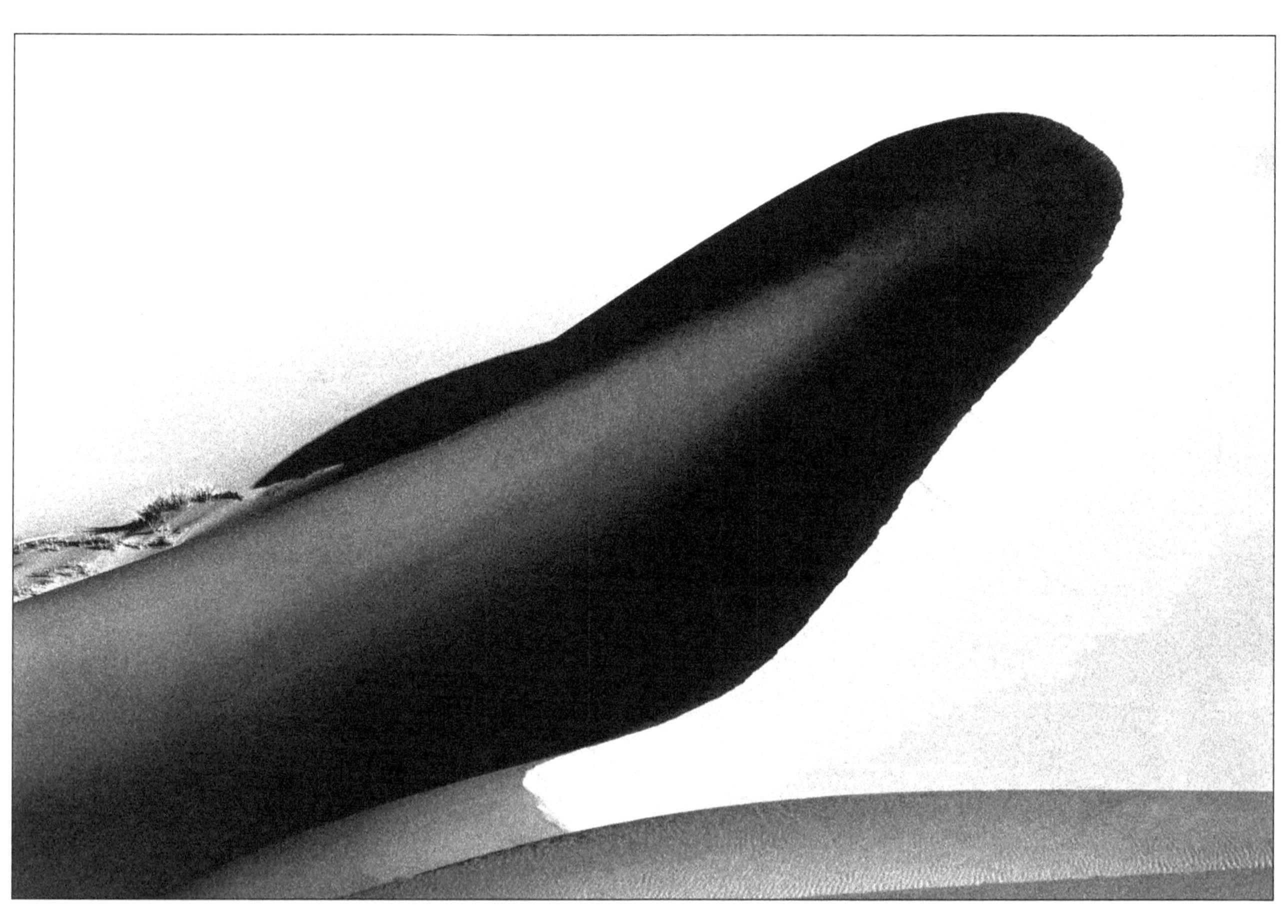

Eureka Springs National Monument, California 1996

RASPUTI'S PENIS

Rasputin's penis was pickled, put on display
in the Museum of Erotica in St. Petersburg.
A maid found it severed from the body after
he was murdered and stashed it before
local crime scene investigators appeared.

It shows up next in a wooden casket,
worshipped as a fertility symbol by a group
of Parisian ladies. I've known women—
and men—like that, haven't you, who worship
that organ as if it were the holy grail?

Misguided women have even been known
to envy the penis. *I'm not coming back
without one,* a friend once said.
But why? That body part can take over
your life, point you in unfortunate directions.

Rasputin's daughter detested the idea
that her dad's member hung loose amongst
these women—she retrieved it, took it
to California with her. Yes, incestuous.
After the daughter dies, the penis turns up

in a velvet pouch at an auction, eventually
makes its way back to the motherland
where the holy relic turns out to be
a pickled sea cucumber—I hate to think
of how they made that discovery.

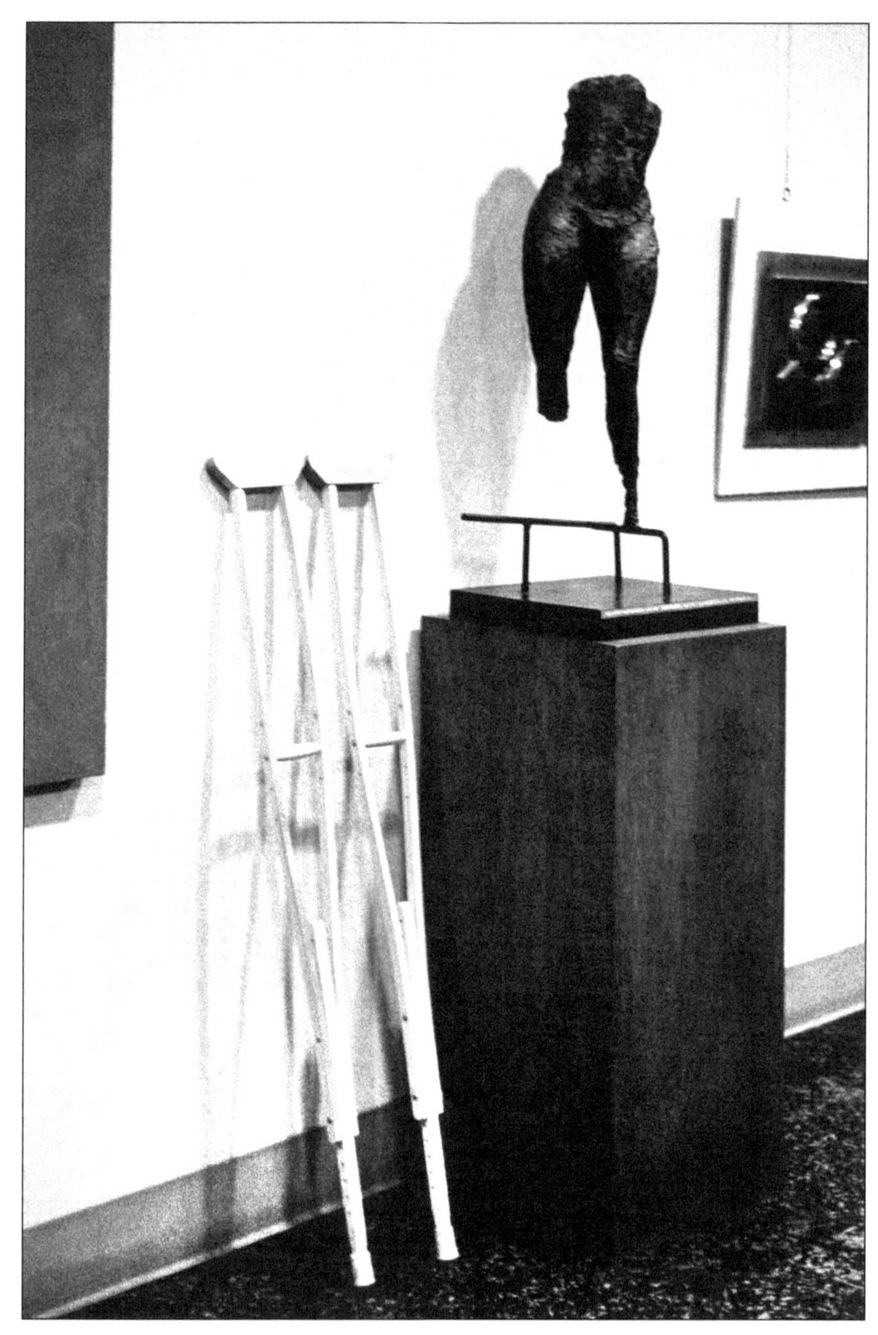

New Orleans, Louisiana 1968

APHRODITE'S HEADACHE

It started with just a finger slashed
opening a jug of wine. Ares had arrived,
bitter and bruised from hours
on the battlefield. After he drinks his fill

I know what he'll want next—I'll have to remove
my girdle, which is getting tighter, harder
to get on and off every year. Being beautiful
has its drawbacks—creatures of heaven

and earth expect me to always look the part.
True I slid from a perfectly scalloped womb,
all long flowing locks and dazed blue eyes,
became my trademark look, but trust me,

I've had to work at it over the centuries—
foundation, powder for pocked skin, blush,
mascara, weeks spent shopping for sheets
to drape just right, everyone thinking I'm a ditz

who majored in make-up at Goddess U.
So when Ares arrives with furrowed brow
wanting a drink, I hurry for the jug and damn,
the stopper is stuck, I can't get it open.

Ares is dozing on the dais, so I grab his sword,
try to pry the lid off and suddenly there's wine
and blood spilling all over. I grab the hem
of my sheet, wrap it over my bleeding finger.

Ares awakens, startled, shakes his head.
By Zeus! he blurts, *you could've just said*
you had a headache, Aphrie. Look what a mess
you've made. And you've wasted all that wine.

Just like a man. What do I have to do
for sympathy here, cut off both my arms?

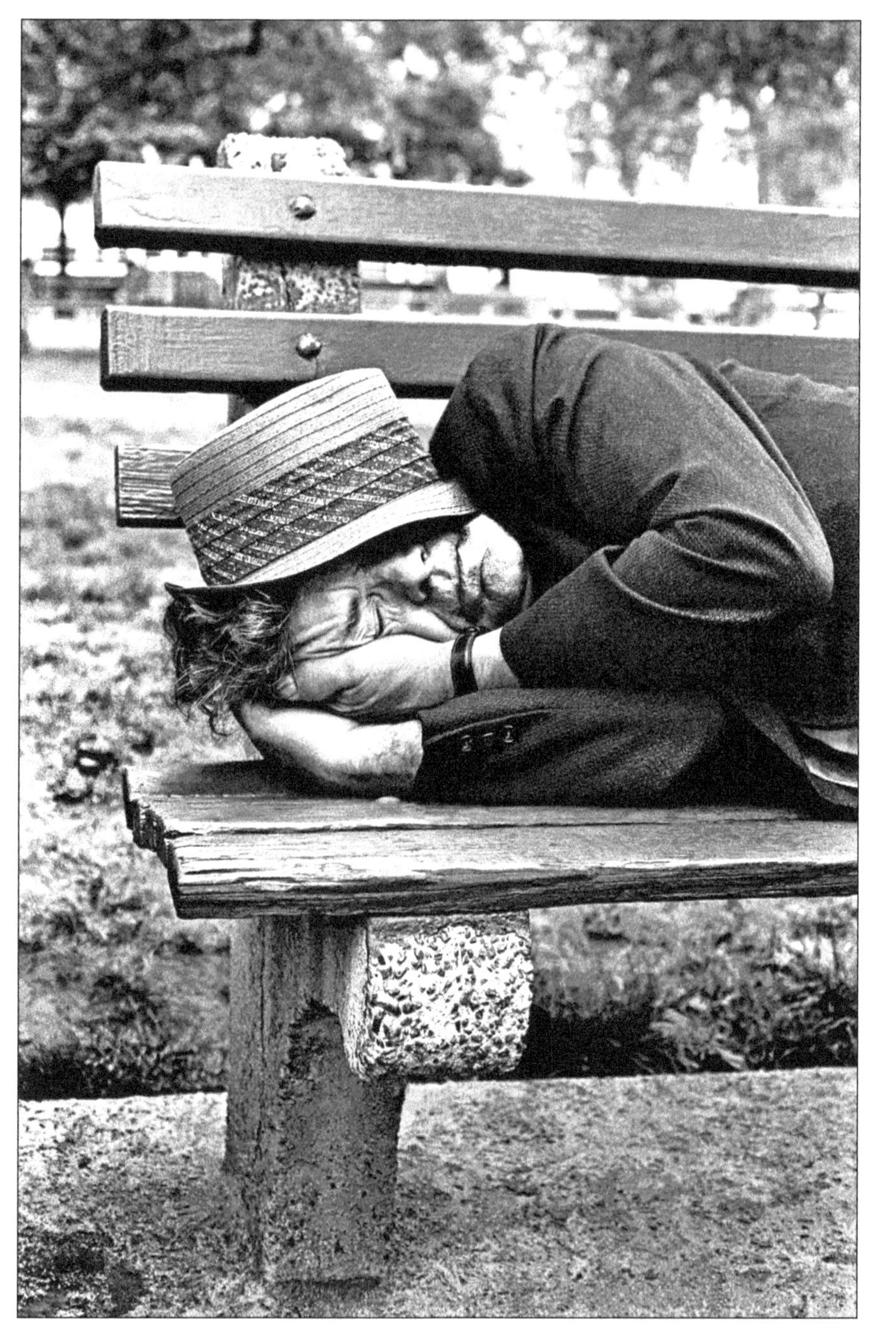

New York, New York 1965

INTOXICATION

I sip from my glass—slim stemmed oval
for mellifluous white, curvacious bowl
for bodacious red—or gulp greedy
from a bottle the way a baby sucks milk

from mama's sweet tit—thirsty bubbles
of amber beer, cool white fire of gin,
liquid gold of a tequila shot,
swallowed neat with a lick of salt.

Don't ask about the reasons I drink—
a lover gone, a leaf falling
from a tree—question only why
I can't stop, the craving passed down

tainting generations—grandma Rose, a splash
of amaretto in her morning coffee, Silver Satin
sipped through the day, my daddy a fall-down drunk,
by night a beached whale outside the bar.

I started at twelve in a best friend's basement,
case of Bud, Rebel Yell, Old Crow on my tongue,
slow melt and burn through my veins,
made me dizzy-sick, but loosened the knots inside,

and still it eases my way through fights
with my wife, nasty boss—a few drinks at night
blows out circuits playing the same tune over
and over—what I did, didn't do, should've done.

Once the taste is on my tongue, I don't stop
until the clutter collides, like marbles spinning
over a slippery surface, sliding off the edge
of my mind so I can start afresh the next day.

I get up every morning, dress, go to work,
stay the day. I'm not some old alkie like my dad—
out of control, on the skids, spouse, kids not talking
to me. It's a habit I can kick anytime.

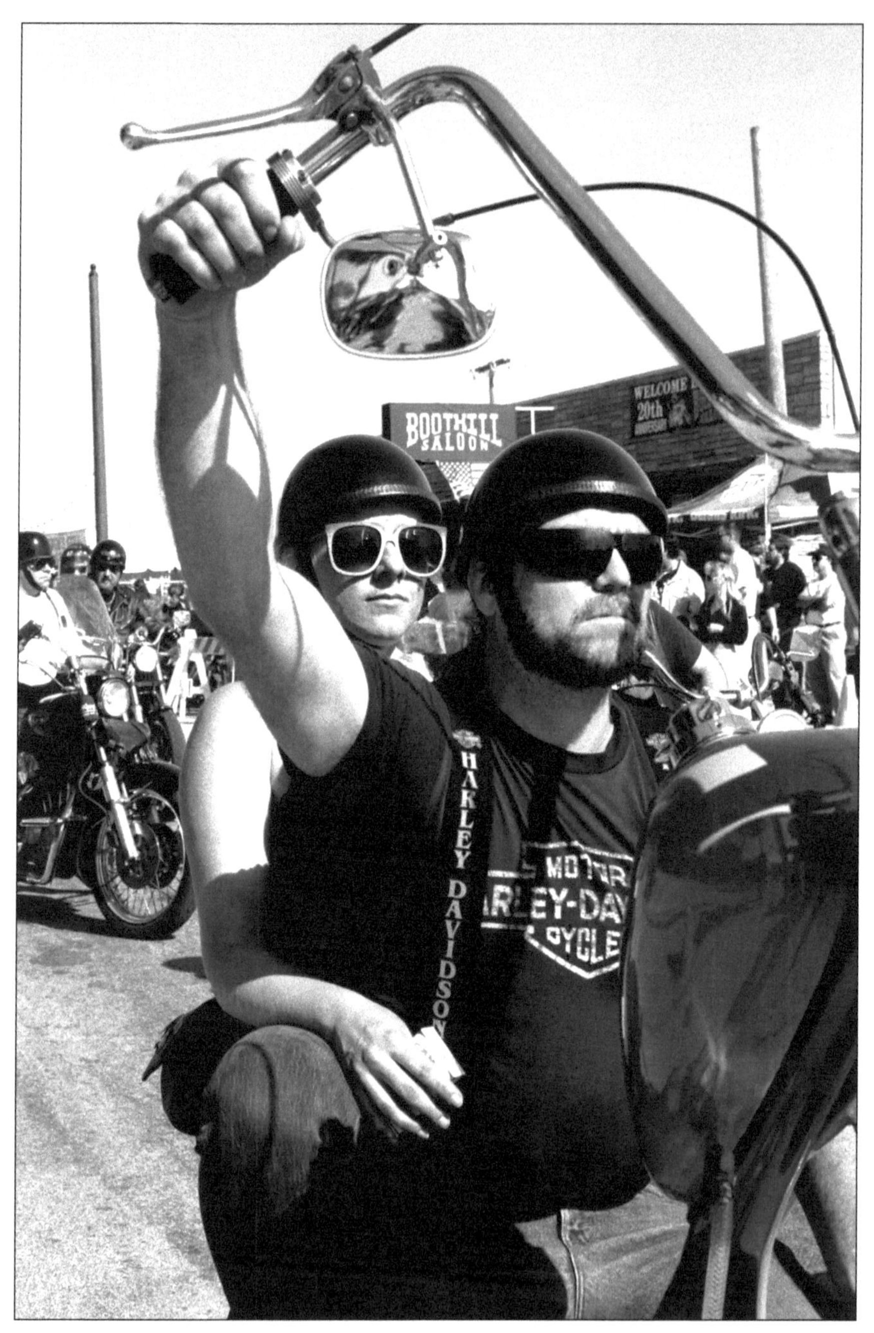

Datona Beach, Florida 1994

READY

--After Sorescu--

I put spikes
on my breasts
made from cactus
sharpened by hail.

I file my tongue
to a dagger.
I paint my skin
and dye my hair
a spicy cayenne.

I race
into town, swing
through alleys searching
for your aching eyes,
your pebbled skin.

And when I find you
I put on my helmet,
climb aboard
and say let's go.

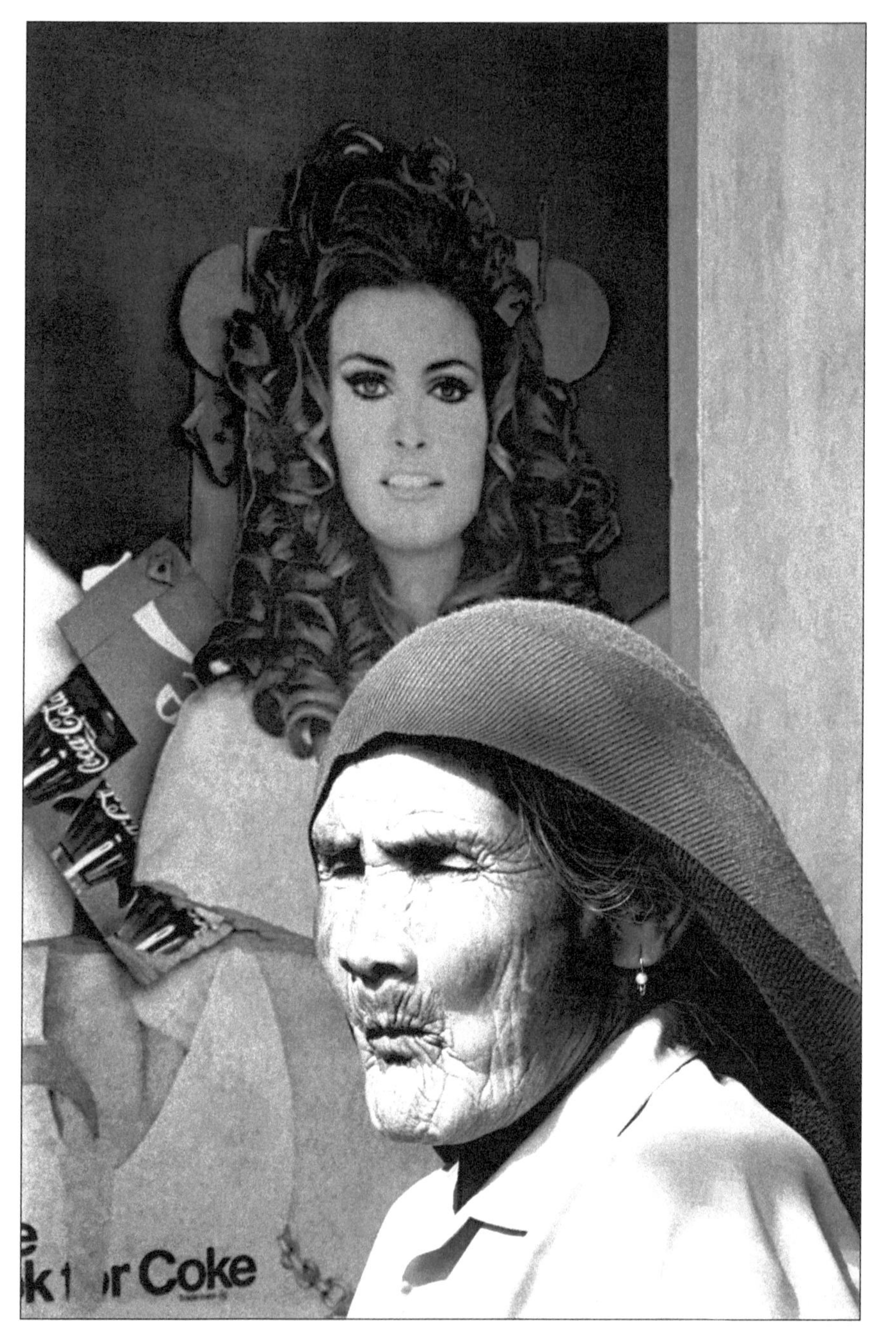

Matamoros, Mexico 1971

MATAMOROS

When I complain about aging,
he shows me a photo he took years ago—

profile of an *abuela* swathed
in black, chin jutting forward,

toothless, hollow cheeks
under high chiseled cheekbones,

black brows like arrows
fierce as a stray wolf prowling

through town, the picture snapped
as she passes under a poster

of a sultry Raquel, eyes ringed
in kohl, whose taut skin

and glossed lips seem to mock
the crone's caved face. He hands me

the framed photograph, asks,
Who is more beautiful?

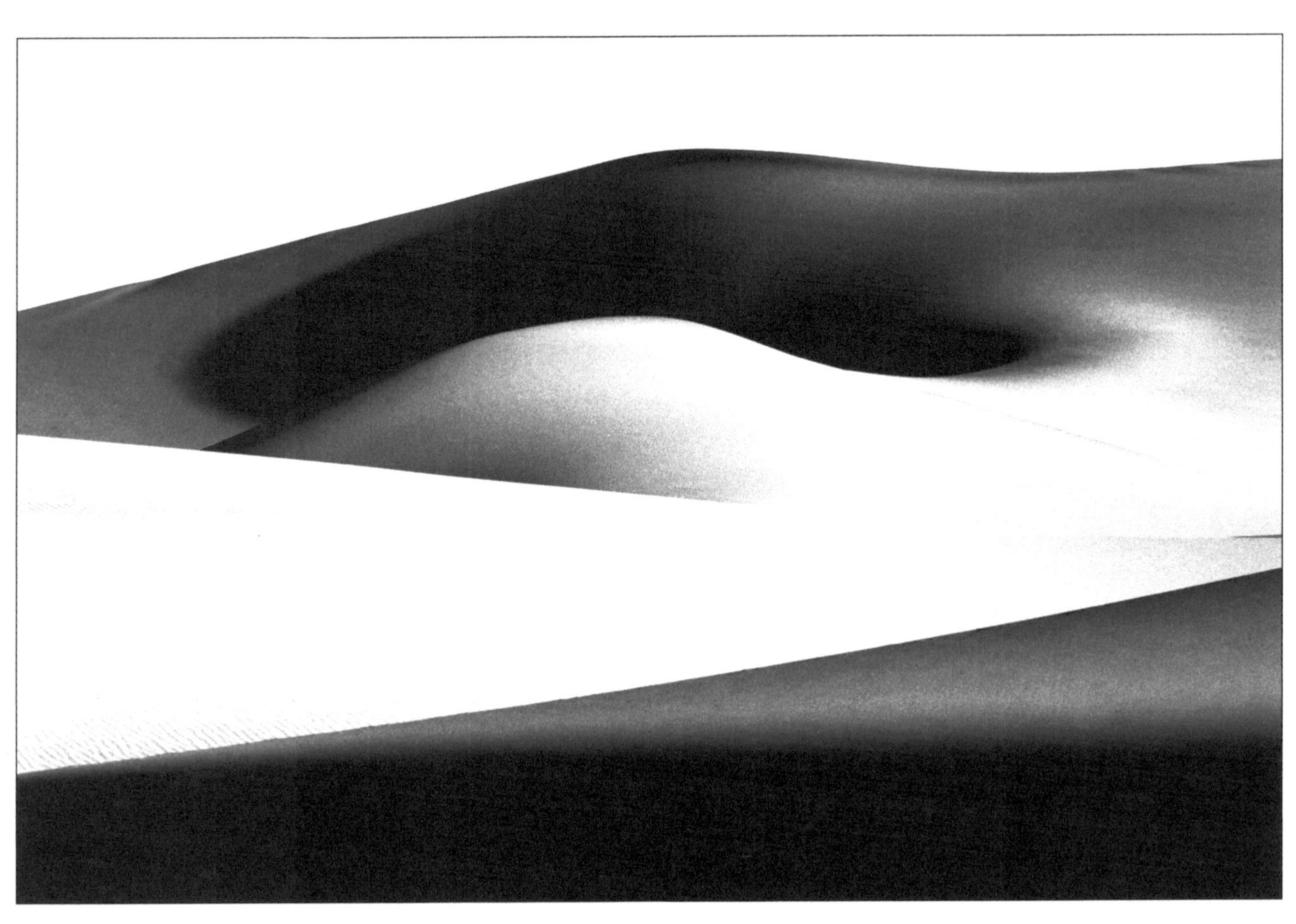

Death Valley National Park, California 1996

DESIRE

Cover my moonstone body
with your obsidian grace

bend, blend, dissolve me
into the heat of desire

before the wind scatters our particles
reconfigures us

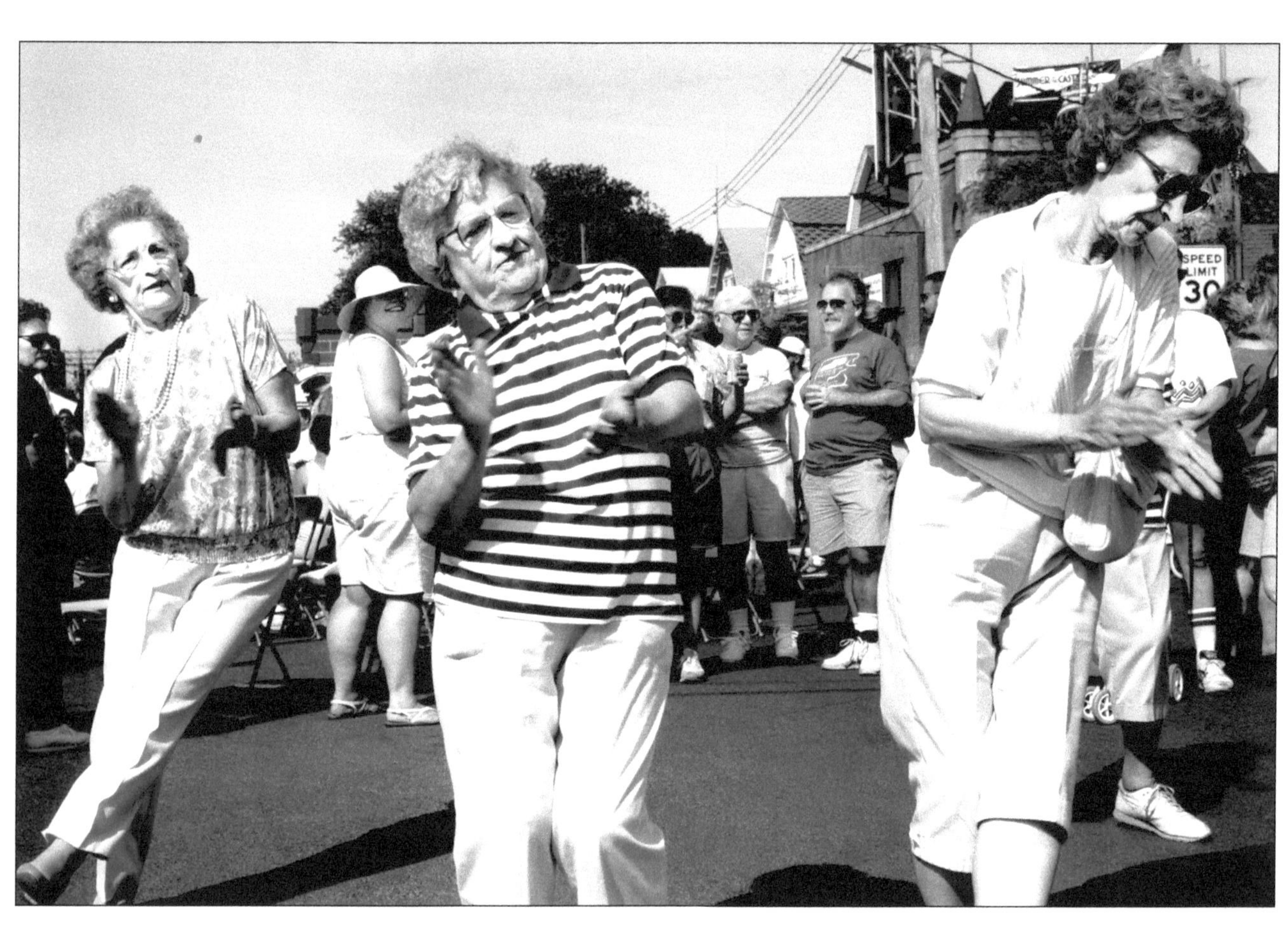

Bridgeport, Connecticut 1993

LINE DANCE

We may not be the Rockettes, but baby
we can still boogie. I remember the first time
I saw those silky legs on stage swing out
in a straight line like grandma's knickers
hanging on a clothesline swaying in a hot breeze.

Mother enrolled me at an early age,
in ballet school, hoping for balance
and poise, although I preferred
the free-wheeling clatter of tap.

I wanted to dance like a showgirl, all glamour
and style, sassy butts bouncing back and forth,
our steps in perfect unison so our bodies looked
like one big wave undulating across the stage.

Backstage I wanted red roses, roving eyes
to idolize my perfect legs, lips, hips. Alas,
knobby knees, weak ankles, cheese doodle toes
prevented a dance career.

My life took a different turn—my husband,
a dour man, refused to dance, so when I was alone
I pirouetted on my suburban parquet floors, broom
in one hand, dustpan in the other, twisted to Chubby

while I dried dishes, shouted out loud with
Ray Charles, and when James Brown came on,
Momma swung her brand new bag around the room
like a lantern in the arc of a shooting star.

It's my time now to dance in a line,
to swing and sway in perfect time—
we may not be the Rockettes
but we can still boogie to rock 'n roll,
swamp pop and cowgirl rhythm 'n' blues.

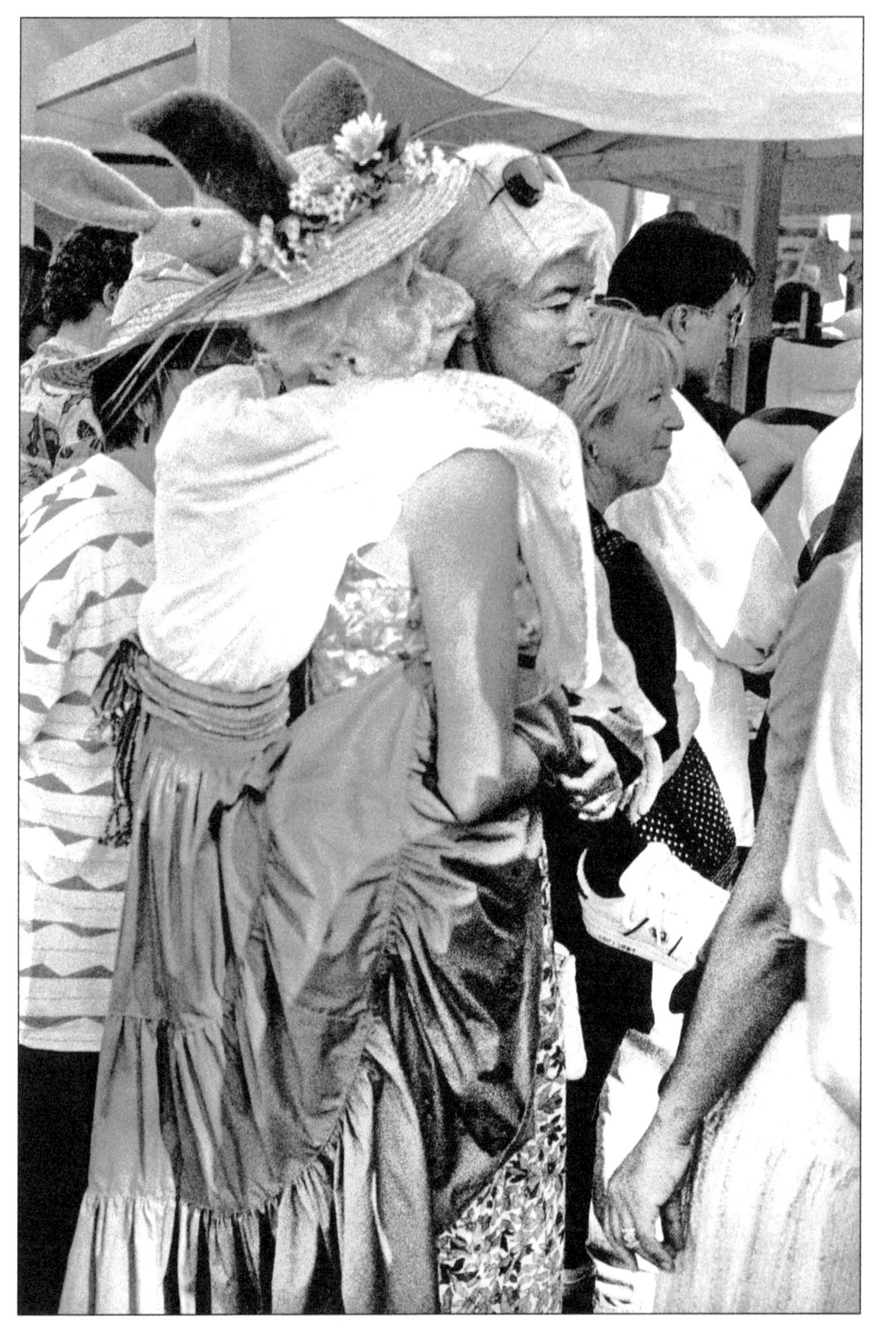

Santa Fe, New Mexico 1992

GHOST OF MY FUTURE SELF

She's not yet the eccentric old lady she hopes
to become before she dies, who doesn't care
if her pants bag out like pajama bottoms

or her hair's a frizzy gray cloud swarming
like gnats around her wrinkled face.
Like every woman she's obsessed with hair—

dye it, go natural, tie it up, let it down, curl,
straighten, bangs, hi-lights, lo-lights, no lights.
It's what we assess every morning,

first thing we notice about each other—
How've you been? Hey, your hair looks good!
Even her patients start their sessions this way.

The obsession shows up in dreams—
she's sitting in the local café in Breaux Bridge
at the Saturday morning Cajun jam, waiting

her turn to sing, suddenly realizes she forgot
to get her hair done—the band stops playing,
and waits while she runs to the hairdresser.

She bumps into Susie, gone from brunette
to golden striped chestnut, who reveals
her husband has prostate cancer,

but the talk quickly switches to whose hair
is too blond—blond says humdrum
like their mothers lying coiffed and dyed

in their coffins while gray says screw it,
this is who I am. Is she ready for that yet?
She considers the cost of a new tint –

maybe it's time to don those baggy jeans,
take up the fiddle, and strum the washboard
with thimbles silver as un-dyed hair.

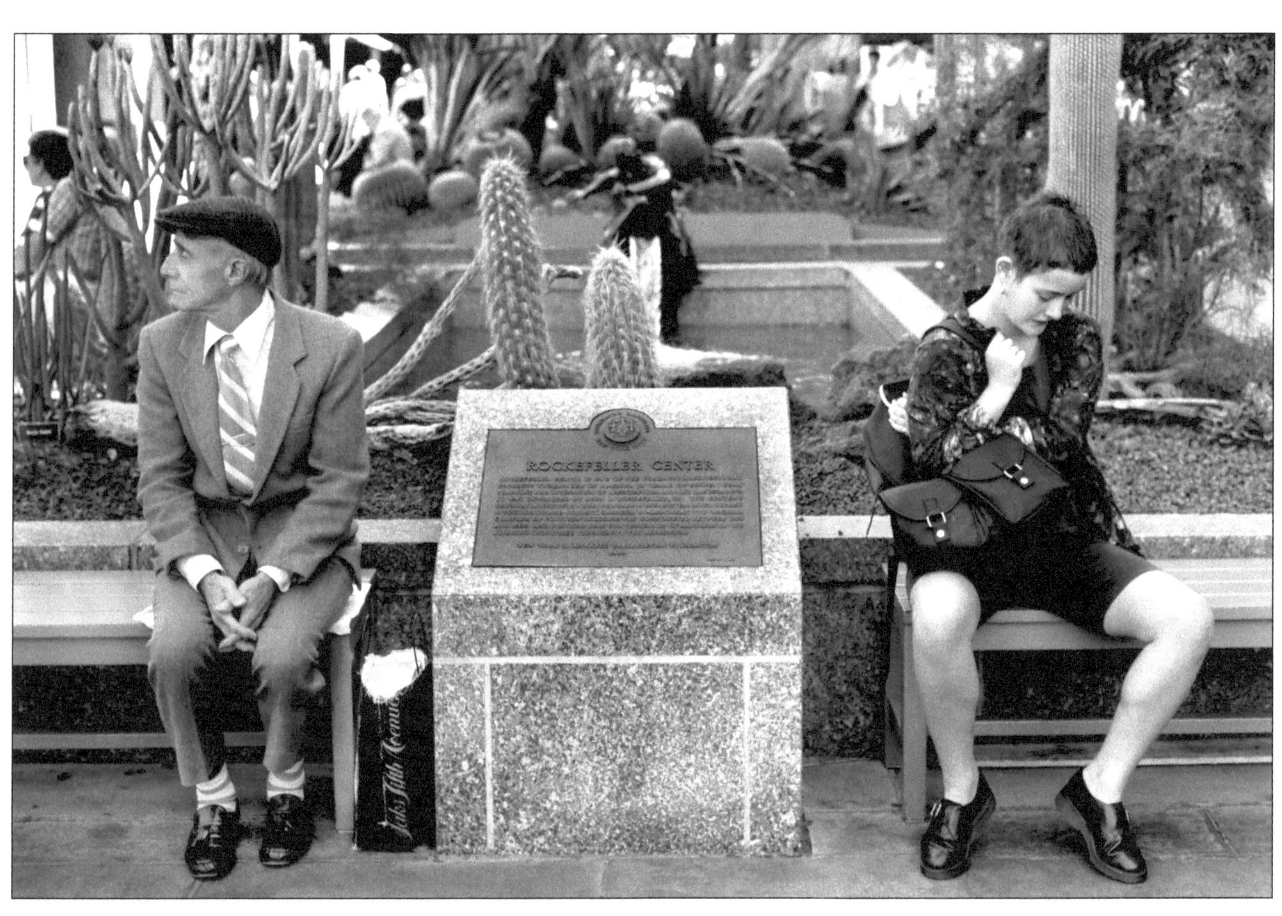

New York, New York 1990

ROCKEFELLER CENTER

The old man gazes
into the distance, waits
for a former self,

a lost companion,
shoulders hunched, hands
clasped between closed knees—

only his brightly striped socks,
matching tie, and the bag by his side
signal that he still shops for hope.

Nearby a young girl sits
gazing downward—an audition
gone awry, a failed exam—her knees

hang wide open, but not inviting
entry, dancer's calves poised
for flight, hands hugging her body.

Old man and young girl sit
on opposite sides of a stone edifice,
stark as a headstone.

Add their ages and divide
by time of day, number of lovers,
lifetime losses. What's left

is the bleak body language
that bridges the distance
between them.

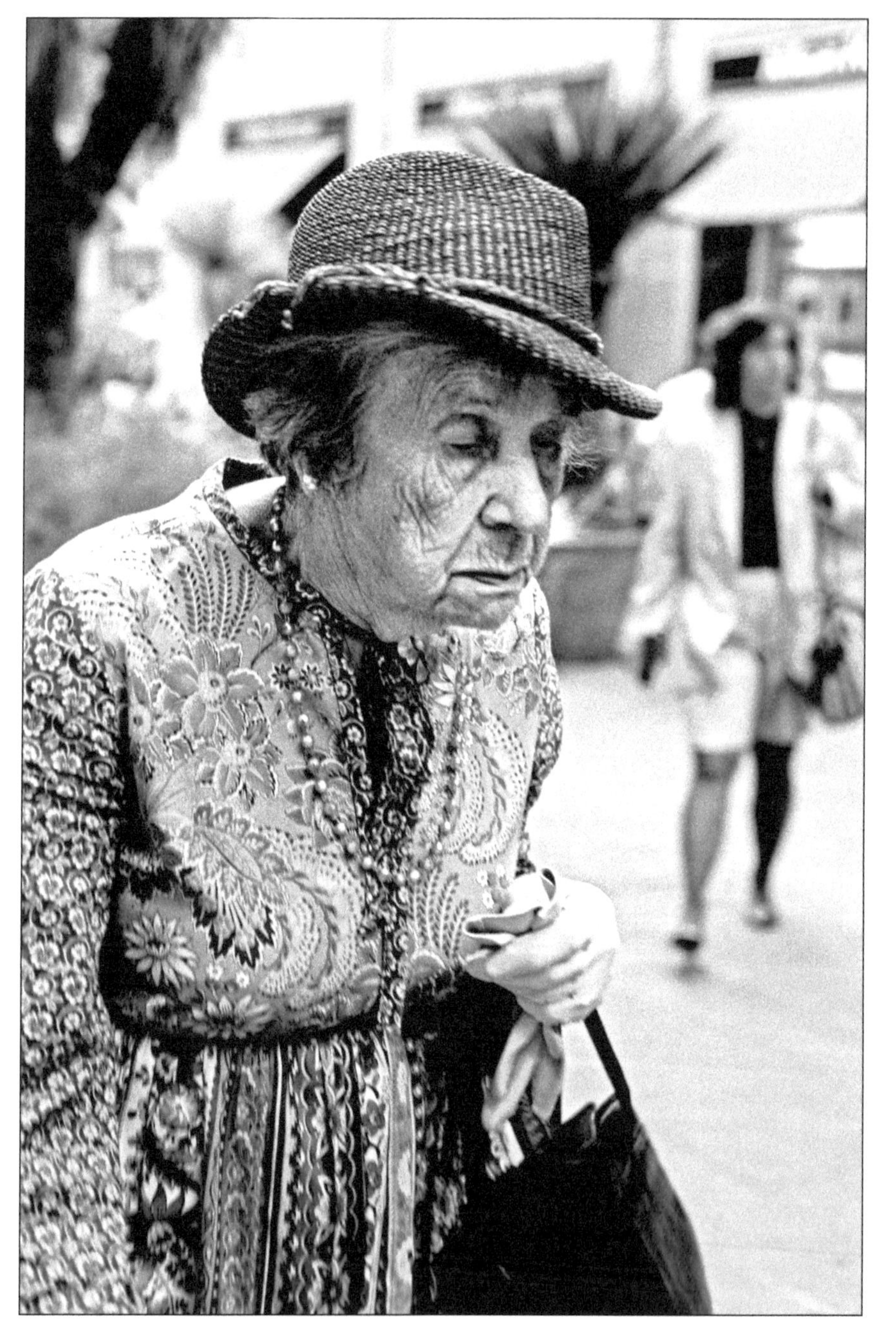

New York, New York 1990

SILK PAISLEY AND PEARLS

A chore, this business
of rising every day,
completing a meticulous ritual—

to wash, to groom, encase
folds of flesh in girdle, garters,
hose, a binding bra—a struggle

for arthritic limbs. Face
powdered, wisps of hair
patted into place, topped

by brimmed hat held
with pins, white gloves
in hand, I descend

into city streets
towards daily chores—
druggist, butcher, banker—

despite losses of family
in the camps, illness,
rampaging age, outlasting all

a dim glory, each step a reprieve
and a reproach, bringing me closer
to those who have left me behind.

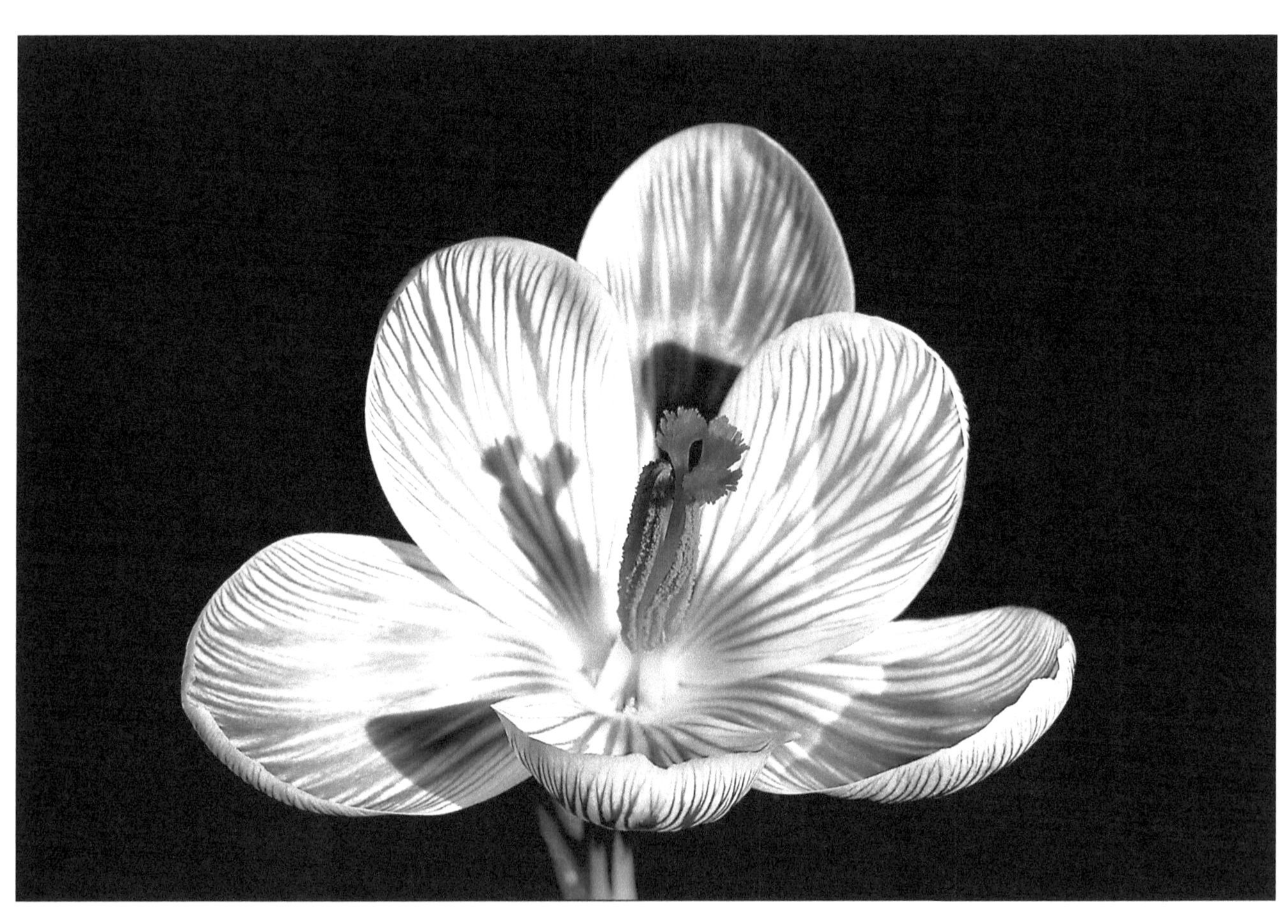

Armonk, New York 2004

THE AGING PLAYER

He's either tilting back
a jug of wine, gulping
whiskey from a canteen
or wailing on the sax—
jazz, rhythm 'n blues
in a neighborhood bar.

He's already made
his imprint, tattooed
silk screen on fickle minds—
he's ravaged angels,
betrayed benefactors,
coasted ruined roads.

Now he longs to lose
himself in the sweet smell
of a flower that will enfold
him all night in her
forgiving petals filled
with morning dew.

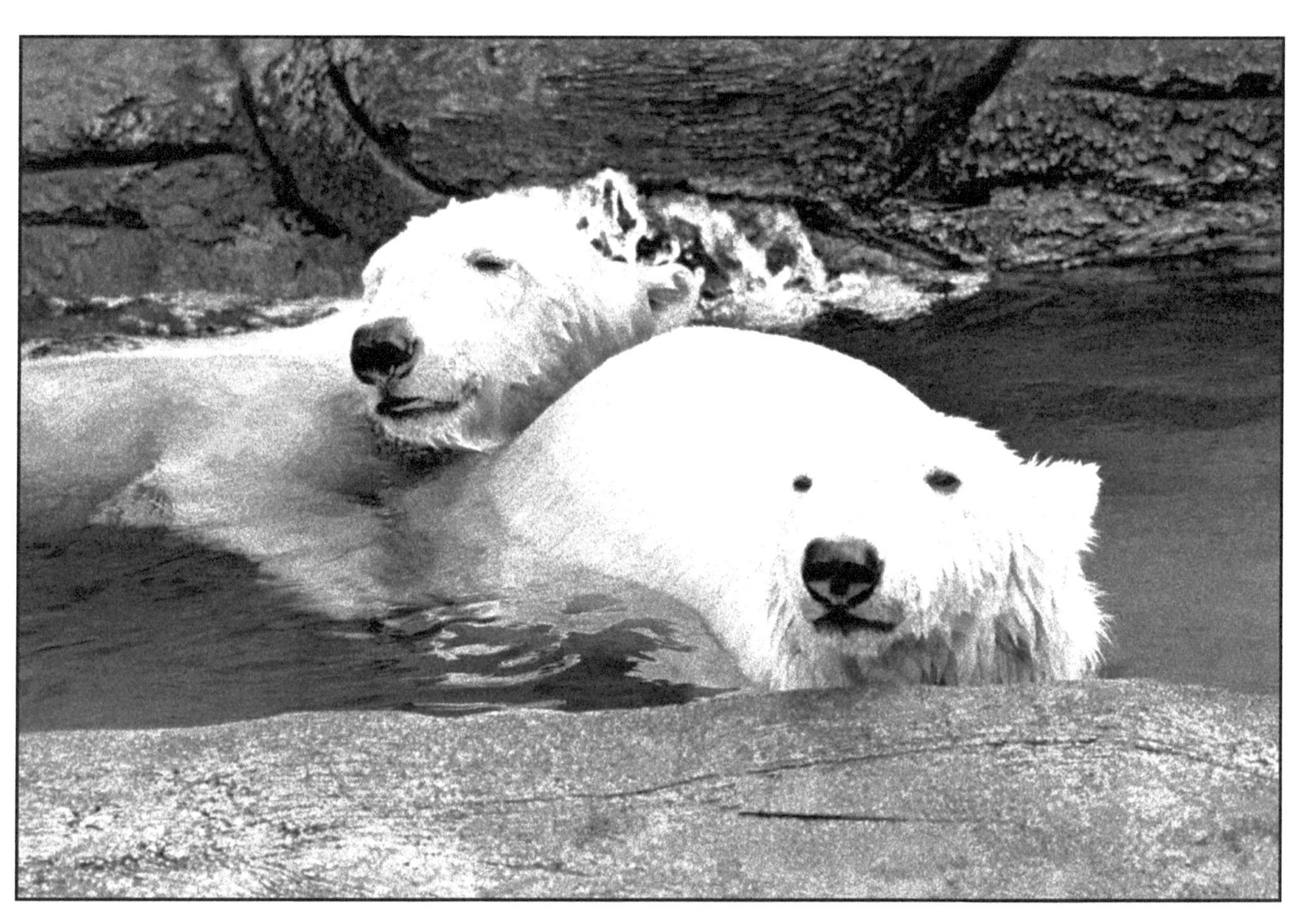

Houston, Texas 1970

POLAR BEARS IN EXILE

She loves the feel of his furry body
 under hers, the textured surface

of their skin, the way she can rest her head
 against his curved back—muscular yet yielding.

Our bodies fit and float in tandem,
 half-submerged in icy water, half-resting on rocks.

Let the world gaze into our glassed-in dwelling,
 think we are robbed of freedom, stripped

of our natural habitat—we have each other,
 safe from the melting glaciers of home.

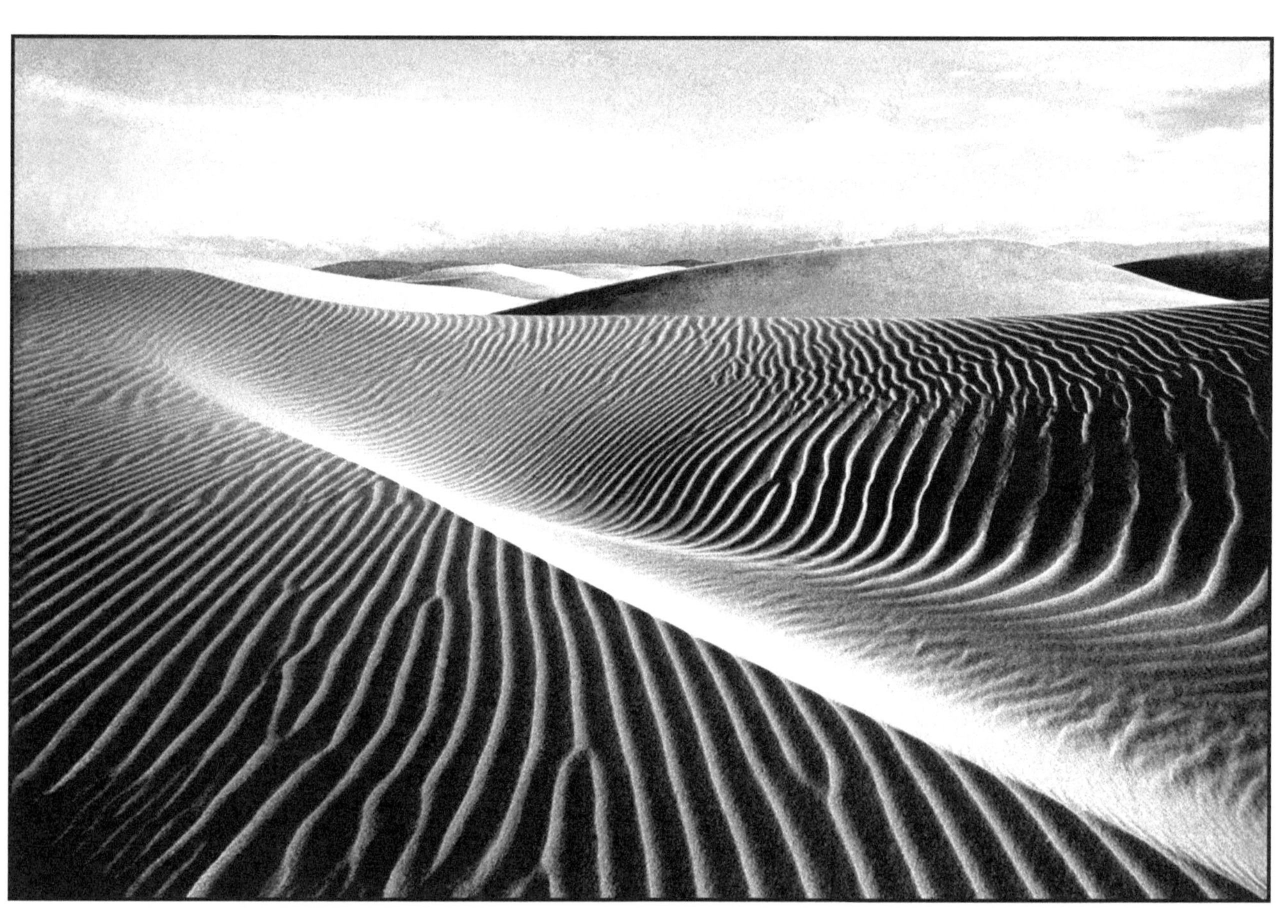

Coro National Park, Venezuela 1993

HORIZON

It seemed as though
a window slid open
onto a buzzing void, singing
songs as fresh as seedlings,
sprouting stars as old as dust,
in dreams that drifted, lost
in a pirogue, dreams
that slumbered, remained
in dusk until we were born.
There was an ember,
a reverie debut, a déjà-vu
that continued and then a sandbox
whose grains mingled and cherfed
and there were birds and burdens born
each instant reveling in and reviling
the muddy earth, grouty mountains,
ice that slid from mittens
knitted and carefully knotted
to not unravel on tiny hands. And
lizards and ants and the holy family
of step uncles and cousins who came
to celebrate the mournful tide,
the oceans sweeping the sand with—
was it joy?

Acknowledgements

Grateful acknowledgment to the editors of the following journals where these poems first appeared, sometimes in slightly different form:

Cadillac Cicatrix: "Autumn In Paris," as "Summer In Paris,"

Learning to Love Louisiana (Yellow Flag Press):

"Hush Over Atchafalaya," and "The Road Widow"

Peacock Review: "Horizon" as "Portal," and "Black On White,"

Poetry Quarterly: "Catalonia, 1973" as "Old Man In a Chair,"

Stickman Review: "Three Nuns,"

Valley Voices: "Line Dance," "Matamoros," "Silver" and "Silk Paisley and Pearls,"

Westview, "The Road Widow,"

Thanks to our friends who offered encouragement, ideas and help with the preparation of this book:

Ellen Devlin, Karen Gershowitz,
Geri Kaplan, Midge Keator, Mara Mills, Rae Taylor.
And the publisher of the first edition of this book, J. Bruce Fuller,
without whose encouragement and support this book would not have been possible.

Photograph Notes

Page **10** -*Photo* **0056 - New Orleans, Louisiana 1969** - *Hitching post tied to tree trunk*

Page **12** - *Photo* **1509 - Atchafalaya Basin Swamp, Louisiana 2014** - *Cypress trees*

Page **14** - *Photo* **0314 - New York, New York 1965** - *Woman with bicycle wheel on a bus*

Page **16** - *Photo* **1171 - Monahans, Texas 1994** - *Monahan's Sand Hills State Park*

Page **18** - *Photo* **1645 - Armonk, New York 2005** - *Cymbibium Orchid Flower*

Page **20** - *Photo* **0040 - Catalonia, Spain 1973** - *Man reading book on sidewalk*

Page **22** - *Photo* **0037 - Honduras, La Ceiba Area 1968** - *Pineapple field worker*

Page **24** - *Photo* **1734 - Monahans, Texas 1994** - *Monahan's Sand Hills State Park*

Page **26** - *Photo* **0305 - Paris, France 1972** - *Street Scene on Left Bank*

Page **28** - *Photo* **0233 - Paris, France 1972** - *Woman on sidewalk on Left Bank*

Page **30** - *Photo* **1068 - Eureka Dunes National Monument 1996** - *Eureka Valley Dunes*

Page **32** - *Photo* **0086 - New Orleans, Louisiana 1968** - *New Orleans Museum of Art*

Page **34** - *Photo* **0309 - New York, New York 1965** - *Tompkins Square Park*

Page **36** - *Photo* **1057 - Daytona Beach, Florida 1994** - *Annual Daytona Beach Bike Week*

Page **38** - *Photo* **0038 - Matamoros, Mexico 1971** - *Woman at food distribution center*

Page **40** - *Photo* **0721 - Death Valley National Park, California 1996** - *Mesquite dunes*

Page **42** - *Photo* **0808 - Bridgeport, Connecticut 1993** - *Annual Lobster Festival*

Page **44** - *Photo* **0539 - Santa Fe, New Mexico 1992** - *71st Annual Indian Market Festival*

Page **46** - *Photo* **0123 - New York, New York 1990** - *Rockefeller Center Plaza*

Page **48** - *Photo* **0573 - New York, New York 1990** - *Rockefeller Center Plaza*

Page **50** - *Photo* **0680 - Armonk, New York 2004** - *Crocus Flower*

Page **52** - *Photo* **2659 - Houston, Texas 1970** - *Polar Bears at Houston Zoo*

Page **54** - *Photo* **0736 - Coro National Park, Venezuela 1993** - *Dunes of Coro*

The Poet

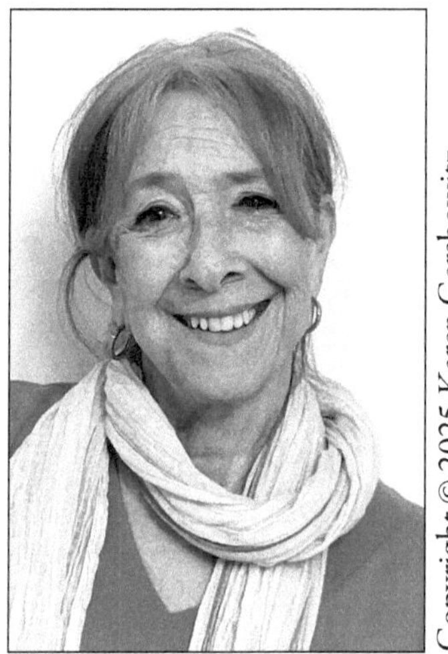

Elizabeth Burk is a psychologist and a native New Yorker who divides her time between family in New York and a home and husband in southwest Louisiana.

Her debut full length poetry book, *UNMOORED,* published in November 2024 by Texas Review Press, is arranged loosely in the form of a memoir describing life growing up in New York City, her experiences as a northerner living in Louisiana and poems on attempting to age with humor and grace.

She has three previous collections: *LEARNING TO LOVE LOUISIANA, LOUISIANA PURCHASE* and *DUET - Poet & Photographer,* a collaboration with her photographer husband, Leo Touchet.

A Pushcart Prize nominee, her poems, prose pieces, and reviews have been widely published in various journals and anthologies, such as Atlanta Review, Rattle, Southern Poetry Anthology, Louisiana Literature, Arkansas Review, Passager, Pithead Chapel, Naugatuck River Review, PANK, Mom Egg Review and elsewhere.

For more information, visit Elizabeth Burk's website:
www. **LizBurk.com**

The Photographer

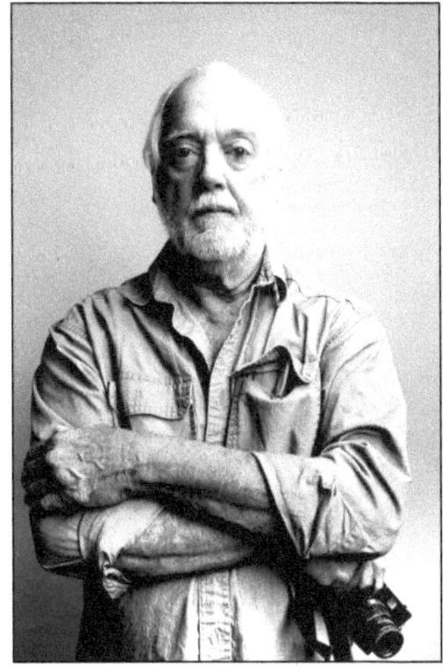

Leo Touchet is a self-taught photographer and native of Abbeville, Louisiana. Following are some of the places his photographs have been:

Books: *REJOICE WHEN YOU DIE - The New Orleans Jazz Funerals,* (LSU Press 1998). Eight books:*PEOPLE AMONG US, AT THE RACES, CHASING SHADOWS*, FLOWERS, CHILDREN AMONG US, THE LIFE OF A DUCK and STILL MOTION with Jiaqing Zheng.

Collections: Sir Elton John Photo Collection, New Orleans Museum of Art, Houston Fine Arts Museum, Bibliotheque Nationale *(France)*, New York Public Library, and other private collections.

Publications: Life, Time, Fortune, The New York Times, The Washington Post, Time-Life books, Oxford American, Der Stern *(Germany),* Panorama (*Italy*) and many other publications.

Exhibits: (Acadiana Center for the Arts-Louisiana), Arizona State University, Everson Museum, Louisiana State University, Mint Museum, Public Theater *(New York)*, Royal Ontario Museum, University of Oklahoma, University of Texas, U.S. Bicentennial Exhibit and *REGARDS et MEMOIRES* (Annual International Photo Expo in Arles, France).

For more information, visit Touchet's website:

www.LeoTouchet.com

ISBN 979-8-9918323-4-2

www.ingramcontent.com/pod-product-compliance
Lightning Source LLC
LaVergne TN
LVHW070148110826
845147LV00002B/350

* 9 7 9 8 9 9 1 8 3 2 3 4 2 *